Art of War in Sino Japanese Wars

ART OF WAR IN
SINO JAPANESE WARS
BY ROBIN SOO

ISBN: 1-4681-3733-6
ISBN-13: 9781468137330
Library of Congress Control Number: 2012900577
Createspace, North Charleston, SC

Art of War in Sino Japanese Wars

Robin Soo

2012

TABLE OF CONTENTS

A Historical fiction on how Sun Tzu's Book Art of War, explains the strategy of Sino Japanese Wars in 1894 and 1937. Attack strategy is used against Warlord Yuan who under the Treaties is supervised by the Kwangtung Army. Militarism uses Military to achieve ends of conquering China. KTA mounts twin Invasion Expeditions to capture Shanghai and Nanjing. Colonel Gary Tang is caught fleeing in the Nanjing massacre, witnessing Kill All Destroy All strategy of war. Sun Tzu advocates capturing the Commander but Chiang evades capture in Wuhan and flees beyond reach in Chungking. A 7 year stalemate ties up a 3 million Japanese Army in China till 1945. Japanese bomb Pearl Harbor conquers S.E. Asia advances on Australia but is defeated by island hopping war.

Chinese Civil War saw the strategy of defend to last man failing to stop the PLA. Also sees strategy of deceptive retreat and surprise ambush by the PLA. Tang retires from Sun Tzu club and shocked to see photos of old Nanjing Massacres being shown to public.

Prologue:

In ancient days a famous General Sun Tzu wrote a Manual of War 'The Art of War.' The military of China and Japan has been influenced by War Strategy attributed to it. This historical fiction looks at the history of the Warlords in China between the years 1895 to 1945. It was a period of Japanese Army expansion in China through military expansion and closely connected to the Sino Japanese War in 1895 and 1937. Acknowledgement is made to a lot of material based on the Internet media www. wikipedia especially the photographs. The work is a historical fiction of the Sino Japanese Wars though reference to historical people and events has also been made. Colonel Tang a student of Japanese War strategies was caught retreating in the Sino Japanese War where the Nanjing massacre took place. He narrates the War strategy of Chinese Generals and Japanese Generals and how the Japanese Army won the Nanjing Battle conquered the cities but lost the Chinese Wars. He criticized the Warlords who were supervised under the Treaties but blames the endemic disunity in China for its own military weakness.

chapter

ONE

Art of War in Sino Japanese Wars

I looked up the grey sky with dark clouds. The War time sky is filled with fear for me as the sight of artillery shells burst into flames when it hits the buildings. The defenders are encircled then shot down by wild charging soldiers of the Japanese Army. I can do nothing to help them but hide in the cave overlooking the small town. The hills in the distant beckon to me as we trudged towards a dark forest with tall trees. We searched for shelter amongst the chalky sides of the sloped land. Where are we? Who are we?

We were the Chinese Army defending Shanghai for two whole months of hard fighting. Then it happened we were flanked by the attacking soldiers who had superior weapons, tanks, ships and artillery but the most vital advantage was their mobility moving troops from one position to another at short notice. As for us we were in a fixed position and we became sitting ducks. Later we were ordered to retreat to join the defenders at Nanjing a march on foot of three weeks.

I remember the outbreak of the Shanghai invasion. We manned the defense station overlooking the Wusong river a tributary of the Huangpu (Whangpoo) river. The Huangpu is a tributary of the Yangzi river as it nears the Sea. We are soldiers manning the fortifications along the grey estuary of Yangzi River fast flowing towards the China seas. A huge long island stands in the center. A few miles upriver we guard the confluence of the Yangzi River and Huangpu River as there are likely landing places for a seaborne invasion force. For three months from July 1937 we stubbornly shot at the invaders as they tried to land and repulsed them. Then suddenly they sailed right past us and took the city upriver. With 500 plane bombers, 500 tanks, and thousands of big artillery guns, they took the city upriver. We were virtually surrounded with no hope of reinforcements. Our Commanders are preparing to evacuate the beloved capital because a one million men army as shown to us through dropped leaflets from the air will attack with fury of the morning sun.

In the book Sun Tzu's the art of war, written some other ancient time in some other ancient war in the years around 482 BC attack is the best defense. It is wise to change your position if a deadly siege is planned by your enemy who has troubled to spend a vast military budget one of the largest in the world to equip a one million men army directed at your throat.

We found a cave behind a clump of bushes and crept in. Where are we? We are somewhere in the foothills a hundred miles short of the fortress city of Nanjing. Our food rations are spare but we shared some tinned food. Far away there were shots in the nearby village and the yelling of Japanese soldiers as they shot and burned their way through the deserted village. Their Divisions and Brigades were on a forced march a scorched earth marauding band of inspired or indoctrinated warriors with one furious aim to take Nanjing by October 1937. The strategic aim is to capture Chiang. If captured make him sign a treaty of restored government then make him as subservient as the infamous stooge of China the Warlord Yuan Shih Kai. I felt happy that Chiang did not keep to his promise to hold Nanjing fort and fight to the last man. At the last minute his advisers listened to an American or western sourced plan to draw the powerful Japanese Army in China towards the far western provinces where their military advantages of Naval ships on the Yangzi, Airplanes, Air Bombers and Tanks are neutralized.

No prisoners will be taken as the Nanjing Invasion Army cannot be burdened with a hundred thousand prisoners of war. A fast moving army light on baggage and sparse food rations cannot be bogged down by winter rains. The ancient war planners has many traditions and one of them is kill and kill all, burn and burn all, destroy and destroy all enemies who fights back. This war cry instilled fear and reduced resistance from local population.

Sun Tzu's book of Wars was written 2500 years ago but the tradition of these ancient armies has been preserved among Chinese military Generals. The first and prime rule the Supreme General is absolute all powerful in War strategy.

The Japanese Generals have their own manuals on the art of war but have preserved their own military traditions. Thus their army is imbued with ancient traditions. Mushashi a famous legendary Japanese Samurai, in 1645 wrote a manual of war called The Book of Five Rings. Although he was a swordsman, the strategy he outlined can be applied to conduct of war.

ATTACK

Once at the enemy, you should not aspire to just strike him, but to cling after the attack.—Miyamoto Musashi,

The moment the enemy relaxes attack strongly and quickly.—Miyamoto Musashi.

When the enemy makes a quick attack, you must attack strongly and calmly aim for his weak point as he draws near, and strongly defeat him.—Miyamoto Musashi,

Attack in an unsuspected manner, knowing his meter and modulation and the appropriate timing.—Miyamoto Musashi,

CHARACTER

In strategy your spiritual bearing must not be any different from normal. Both in fighting and in everyday life you should be determined though calm.—Miyamoto Musashi,

DECEPTION

When you cannot be deceived by men you will have realized the wisdom of strategy.—Miyamoto Musashi,

4

DISCIPLINE When you have attained the way of strategy there will not be one thing that you cannot understand.—Miya-moto Musashi,

But somehow through the warp of time the Japanese Army in China and the Warlord style armies of China retain some of these strong stern military like culture. Winning the war is the prime objective and nothing else matters. Killing is the act of war and burning includes burning of houses as well as dead enemy soldiers. Civilians were killed raped and burned at the height of the war when Chinese resistance did cause a high rate of Japanese casualties. Around August 1937 Japanese Divisions in the Beijing War, and Chahar Wars in North West had encountered stiff resistance and losses were high. Whether this caused the Marauding raping no prisoner taken scorched earth type of warfare in the Nanjing invasion in August 1937 is subject to controversy though I personally believe it did. We witnessed a number of rape murders and mass killings of defenseless civilians. It was a terrible feeling to witness but not able to rescue the victims. The village had a dozen wooden houses next to small farms of wheat. We crept behind a pig sty just in time when six Japanese soldiers strayed into the village. They were drunk with wine and five miles far from their main regiment. From the look on their faces I realized they were out searching for village maidens to satisfy their war lusts. Inside the farm house they dragged out an old man and his old wife.

'Girls where are the girls?' he was slapped hard.

A fat soldier caught the old woman and pulled off her pants.

'No no that is my wife she is too old.' He pointed at the pig sty.

'Banzai, destroy all.'

The old lady's stomach was bayoneted. The old man rushed at the soldier but he was gunned down in cold blood.

'Kill all.'

They encircled the pig sty fifty feet downhill from us. A stray pig ran towards us but they shot it down. Suddenly one of the soldiers grabbed a lady with long hair and shouted 'Koo Niang Koo Niang.'

The other soldiers joined in and gang raped her like wild beasts. After raping her they bayoneted her private parts and stuck a wood into it.

'Burn all kill all. Destroy all.'

It was clear to me now what the three All's mean. After all, the lady was to be killed burned and destroyed. So the act of raping her was an Incidental happening this is war and the Chinese Warlord soldiers should have bowed and respected the war soldiers in the first place.

As if to answer my thoughts, they shouted loudly, 'Banzai Banzai Banzai' which to me sounds like War, War, War.

They heard a whisper of a cry from the pig pen and rushed in with bayonets.

They dragged out three poor creatures in the form of a muddy father, a girl of about fifteen and a girl of about twelve.

'Banzai'' but the poor man swung away and was cut in the side.

Meanwhile another soldier dragged the fifteen year old girl and ordered her to strip. He tore at her farmer shirt and rubbed her tiny breasts laughing and shouting 'Koo Niang Ah Koo Niang Ah.'

The fat soldier who bayoneted her father rushed in and grabbed the twelve year old girl and tore her clothes off then pushed her onto the ground shouting, 'Xiao Koo Niang Xiao Koo Niang Jin Wo Jin Wo.' The sight of the poor tiny girl ravaged by the fat Japanese soldier was unbearable, so I grabbed my pistol and rushed down at them shouting 'Stop it you barbarian soldiers.'

The five soldiers promptly pointed their rifles at my charging figure.

From their flank Major Wu shot three of them with his rifle. He had crept to their rear unable to bear the sight of these rapist murderers. The fourth soldier turned and shot Wu almost six feet away.

Major Wu had saved my life so I shot the soldier who shot him. The last soldier charged at me with his Bayonet but Captain Chung shot him through his head.

It was a horrible spectacle two ravaged teenage girls their father with a bayonet wound to his side, and Major Wu with blood spilling from one of his eyes. Five invader soldiers sprawled dead.

Major Wu looked at the wound of the man with his remaining good eye.

'You are okay man. You must take your daughters to hide in the village to the south. We will lay a trail for pursuit soldiers to the west.'

The man said, 'thanks you have saved my daughters lives.' He gathered them and they fled south.

'Bury the soldiers in a hidden grave. They will surely search for their bodies. Then we must lay out a false trail and hide in the hills. If they can't find us they will resume their advance towards Nanjing.'

Captain Chung volunteered, 'Three of us will lay out a false trail. Take their guns and backpacks. We will rejoin you by radio. Three SOS bleeps no voice calls.'

'Hang on there might be a sixth soldier down at the village,' Major Wu shouted.

We ran downhill looking desperately for a sixth soldier. I remembered the last house they ransacked.

As we searched we came across the soldier sitting on the floor of a wooden house next to the slaughtered bodies of a dead father, mother and child all dead with gunshot wounds. He was an old man looking sadly at his dead victim. He was drinking drunk and mumbling, 'they could be my mother and father. Ah such is life we must obey orders shoot to kill destroy with fire.'

Chung pointed a pistol at the man who seemed too drunk to care.

Major Wu shouted 'hold on he is too drunk. Let us question him.'

'Why do you kill and mutilate civilians? Have you no shame?'

Wu's Japanese was poor so I asked him, 'Did you shoot these three people?'

The Japanese soldier looked weary of life mumbling strange words in his language.

'Ah I failed my duty the sergeant did it for me. But at last I did it kill or be killed, Burn or be burned, destroy or be destroyed. That is our lot. Ours is not to reason why?'

Major Wu looked thoughtful.

'Ours is to fight and die, ours is to fight and die,' the much drunk and gone soldier shouted at the top of his voice, 'kill or be killed, burn or be burned, destroy or be destroyed. I fail to kill I did.'

'Forget him He is too drunk to know what he is doing. He is finished anyway when they find him drunk and with a guilty conscience. They will punish him surely. Let us run and hide.'

Outside as we prepared to go our different ways, a shot rang out from the house followed by a loud cry, 'Banzai.'

Chung saluted Major Wu and Colonel Chu. The three laid trails at the village then headed towards the west. We covered our tracks for three miles then searched for a hideout.

We hid and stayed still. After an hour of wanton killing of civilians in the mountain village the Japanese soldiers heard a bugle and headed for the next village some five miles away.

'The siege of Nanjing is over. The defender of Nanjing was not defeated but overnight he abandoned the city and escaped towards Wuhan. Our plan to join the Defenders at Nanjing is useless now.'

These were the words of Major Wu as he listened to the news by radio. There were seven of us the commanders of Regiment 544. Major Wu looked awkward as he stood there with unshaven face, eye patch and worn civilian clothing which we pilfered from a deserted store. Retreat to Nanjing had been our orders but flee is a better description.

Captain Chung threw a half lit cigarette into the ground. He is the casual type serious at work but happy go lucky at play. He saved me from a bomb explosion when I was wandered away from our Fortifications. I owe him my life so I do not contradict him.

'This is the end for China. They announced no they bragged that their Invasion army would over run our Nanjing government in three months. It is a well planned invasion with two pointed fangs one at Shanghai Wusong which advanced along the shores of the Yangzi Riverside cities towards Nanjing.

By surrounding the defenders with massive firepower unseen in the world they marched behind our flank taking the defensive ports along the Yangzi River. Thus they pretended that their initial attacks were confined to the Wusong Japanese settlement part of International Shanghai. The Chinese defended the Sihang Warehouse to the last man in full view of the foreign powers and tourists. But the Chinese fell for a trap when they counterattacked thinking it was about the defense of the Japanese Wusong settlement. Suddenly they showed their true intention by attacking Chinese riverside cities such as Baoshan and encircled the Wusong Zhabei defenders. Their true objective was an all out invasion of Shanghai then Nanjing not confined to Wusong settlement.

The second invasion force was directed at Su Zhou famous for its supposedly invincible array of five forts. Their Hang Zhou Bay Expedition landed at Hang Zhou Bay. The heaviest bombardments naval warships and air bombardment ever held in China rained on the defenders. Casualties rose by tens of thousands as the Chinese Infantry ordered to fight to the last man or die by the flag. Perhaps it is a gross waste of fighting soldiers but then the Chinese Armies were also descended from an ancient time when the military culture valued bravery more than lost of lives. Sweeping with speed the Invasion Expedition headed by the 10th Army marched speedily inflicting gross terror across the heartland of Jiangsu Province. It killed and burned all life in the simple countryside. We are finished having lost 20000 officers and 400000 men the flower of our army.'

Captain Chung is a brilliant officer who excelled in ambush tactics. Suddenly in less than 60 days half a million soldiers killed or wounded. The intense fighting shook the foundation of this new nation.

We had fought a brave war in defense against the infamous Shanghai Invasion force. We defended against the Japanese charges inflicting heavy casualties. For three months we held our positions. If they charged we defended from behind concrete bunkers then we would charge back at them. Suddenly a non stop barrage of artillery and Japanese bombers from the sky rained thousands of bombs on us. It took three days of bombings then one morning in despair we heard the sound of tanks approaching us. Thirty tanks advanced on our concrete bunkers. Major Wu rang out, 'Commander we have run out of ammunition and we need artillery support against these tanks.'

Colonel Chu roared, 'our orders are to fight till the last man and to hold your position.'

There it was to fight against the wild marauding Japanese army using our hand held rifles. We succeeded in repelling them until their aerial bombings and tank warfare came in. After 24 hours of hopeless defense against the charges by the Japanese soldiers preceded by heavy artillery and tank gunners Colonel Chu counted the bodies of dead defenders.

'60 % of our brave soldiers dead, Ammunition is short as turtle soup and relief units are zero.'

'Maybe just maybe men with ammo running out and without food this position is indefensible. What is your idea Sun Tzu Tang?'

I was lost for words. I replied 'Yes Commander retreat is wise when fighting men face an overwhelming enemy. It is certain death if we sit here without air support and no chance of reinforcement.'

'Action is the mark of War Strategy, not a guy who is clever at talking but never a man of action,' Captain Chung laughed at me in derision, 'Gary Tang you are a good talker but never done anything much more than talk?'

'I am not a Commander, but it is common sense that our Commanders ask us to fight to the last man, but I see the airplanes bomb our bunkers, and tanks fry our comrades with fire, all I have to fight back is this old rifle and not automatic even.'

'Yes, we have received orders to retreat west towards Nanjing our southern capital. Let us run for our precious lives, I say.'

A Small Incident that escalated? No it was not an isolated Incident caused by the shooting down of Lieutenant Oyama. You don't just conveniently place an armada of ships, airplanes, bombers and Landing Craft then land 300000 soldiers on the banks of the Yangzi estuary and then claim it was caused by the shooting of a soldier who shoots travelers at a busy airport.

I looked at my diary and read some of the entries.

The first stage was simple the Chinese Army ordered by Japanese ultimatum to retreat out of Shanghai for shooting Oyama. No rifles or arms allowed by peacekeepers.

Seemingly the war started in July 1937 when a Japanese officer Oyama ran on the roof of the Hong Qiao Airport in Shanghai and started shooting travelers. He was shot dead and the Japanese demanded that the Chinese Army retreat out of Shanghai in accordance with the 1932 Treaty. On refusal to obey their orders which had the same pattern as the Marco Polo Bridge Incident on 9/18 1937 they began a campaign of attack and assault on the Chinese Army.

It was confined to the Wusong river and neighbor district Zhabei but then the Japanese Army expanded the conflict. The Chinese counter attacked and bombed the Japanese flagship but by mistake bombed the American flagship. The Japanese expanded the war zone by landing upriver and encircled the Shanghai defenders. Strongly supported by Air bombers, tanks and artillery, they captured and destroyed dozens of strongholds. With ammunition running out and fixed point defending of posts the Chinese Army lost 80% of many divisions. Poor strategy and false assumptions were leveled but none dared to say it openly. We were simply shell shocked and our minds blank as our eyes stare at dead comrades bodies burned beyond recognition.

My name is Captain Gary Tang. I joined the Regiment 544 last year 1936 when the Neighborhood school in Shanghai conducted a public function to call for funds to save China and manpower to fight the Japanese. I remembered attending the funeral of General Sung who died from an incurable but painful disease in faraway Sichuan. He gave his life for the country and with him was lost 40000 soldiers of the Beijing 29th Army. I joined the Army then.

The Xi An Incident rang a liberty bell across all countrymen, to unite as a country. The bells were ringing loudly when our President Chiang flew home safely from the city of Xi An after he was kidnapped by his subordinate the powerful former Warlord of Manchuria Zhang Xue Liang. It is called the Xi An incident and the whole country celebrated when Chiang after being kept as a prisoner for weeks agreed to sign the Pact. The pact is called the United Front of the Left Wing (Communist) and Right Wing (KMT or National Revolutionary) Chinese Armies against the Japanese army in China in late 1936. How did they the Japanese Army land in China? They won and China lost a war in 1895 the Sino Japanese War then as peace treaty was signed they seized territories in Manchuria, Taiwan and Shandong. From the peace treaty of 1896 they carefully left the Chinese Army Commander Viceroy Yuan in control of China but answerable to them indirectly under the terms of the forgotten Treaty. This man Yuan had already lost a Sino Japanese battle in Korea in 1885 when China came to the aid of Queen Min of Korea. Yuan lost in Korea and the Queen Min died in horrible circumstances when 25 swordsmen searched the palace and slashed her to death. Yuan was in Korea with 400 men as the protector but stayed aside quietly. Her king saddened signed all documents required favoring the Japanese presence in Korea. The Japanese Army kept up the war like momentum against China and felt comfortable fighting an enemy War Commander who they know will never beat them. This losing General named Yuan is a master at personal survival and preserving his private army against the southern Chinese who seek to seize power. To keep Yuan in power was like a strong war ally. Every time he lost he would grant concessions to the Japanese until the routine becomes a formality. Lip service patriot that is what he was called. He cared not much about loss of sovereignty over the concessions he granted. By the standards of Sun Tzu's treatise on the art of war, Yuan is a poor General, but he displayed skills to stay in power as Army Boss from 1895 to 1916. His ability to preserve the reign of the Qing dynasty till 1911 and to preserve the military presence of the Japanese Army in Manchuria served him well till his sudden demise in 1916.

Yuan Shih Kai I remembered staring at his photo as Viceroy of Chih Li (Hebei). He suffered defeat at Manchuria and Tianjin but his boss the 72 year old Marshall Li Hong Zhang was required by the Japanese to sign the Treaty of 1895 on board the ship Shimonoseki. This shamed the Chinese patriots in particular a fiery young man in Hong Kong named Sun Yat San who wrote protest letters to Li Hong Zhang ignorant of the War ready Japanese Army in China. Li's mistake was to trust Yuan as an appointee from his own roots the Xiang Army. China was forced to pay huge war reparations 500 million. When Li requested a reduction to 400 million it was granted but in the night alley in dark Yokohama a grey figure shot him in the eye. Why? Daring to ask for a reduction is the probable reason but he did not die was spared which is a great honor in Japanese ancient times. Li Hong Chang passed from the stage of Chinese military affairs but he symbolized the military backwardness of China compared to Japan as she entered the 20th century.

Figure 1::Yuan Shih Kai www.wikipedia

Yuan as Viceroy of Army was greatly valued by last Empress Dowager Cixi in managing the survival of Manchu Dynasty via treaties such as Boxer Rebellion when she fled her Palace as a disguised peasant.

Figure 2. Cixi Empress Dowager

Figure 3 Cixi Dowager Empress
source: www.wikipedia

Li Hong Zhang the old Marshall, mentored the young emperor Guang Xu to westernize with arms and a western army. When the Boxer Rebellion broke out and the 12 western nations plus Japan vanquished the anti foreigner rebellion and burnt the Summer Palace, dethronement was feared by the Empress Dowager. The Empress Dowager having control of the Palace Guards and the Chinese Army under Yuan Shih Kai then ousted the young Emperor and made him a Palace Prisoner. There were rumors he supported the Boxers. Thus the military power fell to Yuan Shih Kai till in 1908 when Dowager Empress Cixi died. The Japanese Army in China was aware that the military defense of China rested on strongman Yuan a General who honored the terms of the Sino Japanese Treaty and avoided war at all costs. Hence the Warlord period between 1913 and 1928 was one of peace but without honor and with much national shame. Li's attempt at modernizing China's military was moderately successful but nothing compared to the modernization of Japan's military which embraced an army based on the Prussian model and a Navy of battleships and later aircraft carriers.

Figure 4: Marshall Li Hong Zhang.
Source: www.Wikipedia

Japanese Army Presence in China
The fruits of Li Hong Zhang's army modernization led to the rapid personal rise of Warlord Yuan from 1895 to 1916 when he

died. Yuan pretended to support the Rebellion of Sun Yat San in 1911 but with Yuan's control over the army of the dethroned Emperor he out maneuvered the civilian cabinet until 1913 when he became self appointed President of China. Sun was forced to flee to Japan in exile. In 1928 the army of Sun who is recognized as founder of modern China but who died in 1925 was commanded by his army adviser General Chiang. Chiang used a gunboat in 1924 to rescue Sun from a Warlord and gained his trust as KMT President. Chiang's government is only 9 years old in 1937 but it had faced a series of tests such as 1928 assassination of Warlord Zhang Tso Lin, 1928 Jinan Incident Shandong, 1931 Mukden Incident when Manchurian armies were expelled, 1932 founding of Manchukuo a taking of Chinese land, 1932 Shanghai War, 1937 Battle for Beijing/Tianjin, and Chahar wars and currently Shanghai Invasion and Nanjing invasion. And now Japan Army is prepared to throw away the veil of secrecy to openly conduct war and capture Nanjing the southern capital aiming to install a friendly Chinese government.

Military expansion

For 40 years from 1895 the Japanese Army in China increased their power in North China north of the Yangzi River. By 1928/1931 they drove the Manchurian Warlord the most powerful army in North China out of their remaining garrisons in Manchuria. Like the predictions in Sun Tzu's book of Wars the Japanese Army in China practiced the Art of War on foreign shore. The most vital strategies of war they mastered with ease.

'Waging War requires winning decisive engagements quickly. This requires limiting the cost of competition and conflict. Towards this end they deployed two columns of invaders supported by navy, tanks and planes. Why? Achieve victory with speed.'

Our destination Nanjing is impossible.

As I talked Captain Chung grew impatient. We are being pursued by deadly and victorious Japanese. Where shall we go? We can go out west to Chungking?

'Nonsense, Tang. The eruptions were small scaled Incidents such as the Marco Polo Bridge Incident 9/18 which grew out of control. If we are not forced to hide inside this rat hole I would go out for a walk.' Chung protested out of sheer boredom.

Colonel Chu spoke out, 'Today we hide in defeat to save our lives. All over China small groups of simple soldiers like us wonder aloud 'what Japanese tornado hit us? Was it not our army leaders that lost us this war? They forgot to buy arms and war machines preferring to rely on manpower.'

'Let me finish. Are we not asking why the Japanese Army in China uses the knowledge of Sun Tzu's Strategies of war against us? Four other strategies they have applied against Chiang our supreme commander.'

Let me turn to the use of spies and traitors in the art of war. A strange incident happened when President Chiang returned from the Xi An incident. Chiang's plane approached Nanjing Airport when the lights of the runway were suddenly turned off. In pitch darkness the plane circled the airport losing fuel. Who caused this Incident if not a spy or traitor? The plane was saved from a fatal crash as hundreds of Madame Chiang's friends drove their cars to the runway and turned on the lights.

I was drinking with my friend David Kung in our favorite nightclub.

'Have you heard the Xi An incident has pitted friends against friends? The issue is whether Chiang should order Young Marshall to hunt the Communists down when his heart is bent on fighting the Japanese who over ran his former Province Manchuria.'

A couple of ladies in tight fitting Qipao or cheongsam joined the next table. I spotted this girl I forgot her name a tall girl with long hair with an oval face and a sweet smile. Her companion a medium height girl turned around and shouted, 'Hi David who is your friend?'

David introduced me, 'Hi Gary this young lady is Maggie Kung my little sister, and this smashing girl is Grace Lu her best friend and my cousin sister. Ladies Gary is just returned from America and is a businessman who operates in Shanghai and Nanjing.'

It appeared to be a prearranged thing as David grabbed my hands and we joined their table for dinner. He fell for Grace and talked to her with attentiveness. Grace was polite but retained a cold formality which made it difficult to talk about her personal life.

Grace announced, 'tonight something important is going to happen. Our President who was kidnapped in Xi An has been freed and will return by plane tonight. David and Gary if you have motor cars I fear we may need your cars to provide for runway guide lights at the airport.'

'Sure, I will join the procession of cars to provide headlights.'

David asked, 'Why is it sabotage or work of spies?'

Grace said, 'thanks be at the airport at 11pm use the code word Airport Lights. Spies are everywhere we were warned by our Secretary in our small book club. '

'I will do anything to save our President Chiang and the Young Marshall if they return together.'

Grace shook my hands then David's, 'thank you thank you our country needs people like you.'

I confess Grace was attractive something in her smile struck me. Her background was poor but she made it with the help of Maggie's mum who ran a business selling ladies dress and high class jewelry. Grace had a natural air of beauty mixed with a talent to help her clients. She made herself a popular consultant among the rich and famous ladies of Nanjing city.

Two hours later I stopped my car behind David's. Grace was in David's car and Maggie in mine. We saw the airplane arriving from Xi An but as it circled the Airport the runway flood lights were switched off. In pitch darkness Maggie shouted, 'Will the plane crash?'

Grace shouted back, 'line up your cars along the runway. As suspected there are paid Japanese spies trying to sabotage our leaders.'

It was a wonderful sight as we watched the plane landed safely in Nanjing. I felt proud of myself and impressed with this girl Grace Lu beautiful and a great leader. If not for David I could easily have fallen in love with her.

Grace thanked us in these words, 'Madame Sun Yat San and her sister Madam Chiang were worried about the safety of our President. I work for them through Maggie Kung's mother, her name is Elizabeth Kung. We thank you from the bottom of our heart. I could not imagine what blow we would have suffered if the President's plane had crashed.'

I watched in admiration as she looked very efficient and attractive.

Chiang had many rivals in his own military and someone was disappointed when the Young Marshall did not take his life but instead accompanied Chiang back to Nanjing as his hostage. Marshall Zhang Xue Liang who kidnapped Chiang and demanded he has to sign the United Front. He begged Chiang to sign the United Front against the Japanese Army in China and offered the term that he became Chiang's self volunteered palace prisoner. Young Marshall was on the airplane. The plot which was suspected was as much to finish him as Chiang in a fatal crash. The use of a Plane crash on which the victim travels is an old spy trick to get rid of an ally who has proved an embarrassment. No doubt this method will be used in the present and in the future.

Xi An Incident Chiang kidnapped

The background is important. In 1928 Young Marshall had ordered his father Marshall Chang Tso Lin's Deputy a man named Yang Yu Ting shot for suspected involvement in the train explosion which killed his father Chang Tso Lin. It was called the Manchurian Incident of 1928. If the airplane in 1936 had crashed killing Young Marshall Zhang and Chiang, it would have been an example of Sun Tzu's strategy of using spies and assassinations to sow confusion in the enemy. The most likely beneficiary of this attempt would have been the rise of Wang Jing Wei as President as he had in 1932 already set up in Guang Zhou a rival government to Chiang's Chinese government at Nanjing. Wang is a relic of the past a Confucian gentleman who loves the Chinese land and gentry culture in an era where the peasants starved and demanded drastic change. They accuse the Gentry of land ownership practices and corruption at the top levels. Wang was Sun Yat San's deputy and fought to be Sun's successor. At the best he could only deal with the Japanese Army in China as a civilian vassal for he is not a military man. Fighting the Japanese is a military task.

It was a rare instance of brief national unity when Madame Chiang's sister the widow of Sun Yat San sought the help of the Leftist Army. Personally the Secretary of the Leftwing Movement a selfless legend named Zhou En Lai flew to Xi An and signed the United Front Alliance. The Nation united under Chiang.

The rest of our group spent their day doing nothing but Chung and I started a group to discus Sun Tzu's approach to war.

Chung challenged my views, 'Your telling us of the Xi An Incident is not related to our Nanjing War.'

I replied, 'If the Manchurian Army of 1 million men, joined the Japanese Army in 1936 Chiang's army of 500000 would be driven out of Beijing.'

Chung remained silent as a hush fell on our members. 'Why? why then did the Young Marshall declare that his Army's flag will fly under Chiang's?'

From my diary I showed them a picture of Chiang under the control of the stern looking Manchurian Generals. A thin looking Chiang and standing next to his kidnapper Young Marshall Zhang Xue Liang. What I saw was determination in his eyes to help China unite and fight as allies. I sympathized with him knowing that the Japanese Army had been implicated in the train explosion in 1928 in Mukden Manchuria that killed his father. A most powerful Army head in the north, he was swept aside by the Beijing Tianjin Invasion of Japanese Army in China. His tragedy was shared by all Chinese brave hearts. Even a powerful and feared Warlord's son can be betrayed by traitors inside his armies. He led a happy go lucky life with Warlord Zhang ZongChang. Now in the Xi An incident he is a symbol of China's search for National Unity in the face of Japan Army's powerful presence in China.

Figure 5: Xi An Incident Dec 1936 Zhang Xue Liang and Chiang. Source: http://history.cultural-china.com/en/34History7514.html

Captain Chung stopped hiss bored look, listened this time with interest. Captain Chung condemned the unknown rivals of Chiang in these words.

'China's military is always split by factions and regional Warlords who do not easily obey a central army Commander like Chiang. Throughout Warlord era internal power struggles and cliques have been seen in Chinese politics. The most infamous internal politics was seen when the founder of the Tang Dynasty Li Shih Min or emperor Tai Zhong was ambushed by his own elder brother Crown Prince Li Jien Cheng. Li Shih Min plunged a sword into his brother's body.'

Sun Tzu warned against this trend to form cliques and factions within a unified army. Sun Tzu wrote a military manual a very long long time ago in the years of the Autumn and Spring centuries in Chinese history. It was the years between 650 and 482 BC. Cliques were formed during another later Chinese era. Qin Shih Hwang Ti was the epitome of the art of war. Absolute power and personal power lay at his hands and the State was indistinguishable from him. He was ruthless and acted for the good of the state but when he died a hundred rebel commanders swept his son and heir from power. His elder son and his strong General were forced to commit suicide by a will forged by Li Si his mentor minister with connivance of Cao the chief eunuch. The First Imperial court saw courtiers plotting for power and corruption. Yes Chinese history shows that the rise of a Dynasty is about war whoever wins by force becomes all powerful and autocratic using the sword to achieve obedience and loyalty. The practice of I win you lose you lose your head was born in those times.

I ended my talk to the cave we were in by saying, 'the mark of the ancient army is the Commanders absolute power. He is the Emperor and autocratic commander.'

Colonel Chu and Major Wu our senior officers changed the subject, 'My family is stranded in the village near Su Zhou. I pray they are safe from their mad slaughter.'

Major Wu disagreed with my views.

'Autocratic power by a Commander is good for fighting battles. But winning is even more important. Chiang has autocratic power but the problem is how to win? He needs to weld them together. The examples of the heroes in the Three Kingdoms prove that their natural loyalty to each other and their oath to defend each other in battles gives them an inner strength. The bonds of war gives an army inner strength. The Left wing or PLA has bonds built up from their survival in the Long March in 1934. I heard the Chu Mao bandit twin leaders started as a small band of bandits. They copied the ancient bandits who hid in the western Margins and applied stories about the martial strategies of these famous warriors to guide their battles and protect each other. From this simple blood oath they somehow started the practice of a commander working with a commissar to settle strategies. Basically it was a matter of survival in the early days the meeting of a pragmatic former warlord soldier and an idealistic librarian. How is that for strategy?'

I retorted, 'KMT Generals of ours have Warlord backgrounds. How do you get them to bond with tank warfare, aerial warfare and naval warfare? Impossible? They know infantry but nothing else.'

Major Wu laughed but agreed with me.

'I suppose like the Boxer warriors in the Boxer rebellion, magic incantations, bodies that bullets cannot kill. These brave Generals have no hope fighting the Japanese armored divisions. Maybe the Americans will provide air cover.'

There followed a long silence. We stayed hidden in the cramped cave for four days while the Japanese regiments hurried on feet and small cars towards Nanjing. I started to talk as things got bored doing nothing. We knew that in the day we must hide.

'Bear with me we will be able to start walking again tonight. It's best we walk southwards towards Hubei or Hunan where it's safer. Today General Chiang is faced with a greater challenge and danger. The rise and rise of the Japanese Army in China as it seeks to play one Chinese Warlord against another.'

Chung was bored. He commented, 'today the Japanese rule Manchuria, and is invading Beijing and Chahar after they have tied up the Warlords of Shandong, Hebei and Henan. Disunity is the real state of nature. For the new President Chiang to claim that he rules the united whole of China is simply not true.'

Major Wu looked with anger at Chung and turned towards Colonel Chu.

'Colonel Chu, we are the government of China are we not? Chiang has a united government no?'

'I have been a soldier for a few years but I have always observed that each Chinese Warlord pays lip service to their central commander but takes care to preserve their private and personal army. Our Commander Chiang is not a Warlord but many of his allies are former Warlords who take care of their own private army. Look at Warlord Yan Shi Shan of Shanxi. He is an ally one year and no more the next. His private army comes first. Luckily Chiang has his Whampoa trained Generals as the back-bone of the Army.'

Colonel Chu looked at Chung disapprovingly.

'The Japanese Army in China is highly disciplined and each soldier is indoctrinated to destroy the enemy and overcome the foe. Look at Captain Chung if he speaks so ill willed against his own army inside the Japanese army he will be shot. But in Chinese circles he gets away with it.'

We are upsetting each other. Chung spoke in a soft kind voice, 'I saw with my own eyes 10000 soldiers trapped in a war trench. Then 10 airplanes swooped down with two dozen bombs, and then they are gone. Some of them were my best friends. Next the Japanese Tanks rolled through the trenches firing powerful machine guns at the remnants of a battalion of men. We need planes and tanks but it is a useless dream at this late hour.'

At that moment there was a sound behind us and five Chinese soldiers wandered near our cave. They begged us for food and permission to hide with us. We gave them two tins of food plus some wild vegetables. After an hour we resumed our discussion on the Japanese invasion.

I gave my views. 'Let me explain there are three different matters connected to this invasion by Japan and our country's weakness and strengths. First China has two Different Armies making Chiang's leadership difficult. Second is unity dependent on one leader or two?

'Top military leaders in China have tried to westernize with western weapons of war. But they have failed. Li Hong Zhang tried to form military schools, purchase state of art weapons and train in military strategy. But today the Chinese Army whether it be army of Warlords or army of Chiang is comprised mainly of infantry. In contrast the Japanese Army in China has equipped their army with Naval Ships, planes, Artillery and tanks. They fight with unison. So how can we the foot soldiers fight against them with machines of war?'

We shook our heads. Thirdly our job now is simply to survive but hope to fight another day.

'By 1936 the Japanese military in China had organized their Warlords well. The 1935 military agreement called the Ho Umezu pact gave local Warlords legitimacy. General Ho agreed that the major states surrounding Beijing, namely Hebei, Henan and Suiyuan was left to their local Warlords but who were in fact Japanese Army allies. Shandong home of Confucius had a Japanese puppet Warlord Han Fu Qu. Half of China the Northern Half is under the Japanese Army in China.'

Major Wu branded me 'the Sun Tzu strategist of war.'

'The Japanese government in Tokyo has always been friendly to China your suggestion that the Kwangtung Army in China seek control over North China is ludicrous. These Incidents broke out of control fanned by the Chinese soldiers.'

These discussions kept me going as we walked all the way towards the new battle lines.

Chungking Diary

After three weeks of walking we reached Wuhan but then we learned that Wuhan is going to be attacked by the Japanese Army from two pincer movements. One pincer is from Nanjing in the east and the second pincer from Shansi in the north east. The city was in confusion with some regiments preparing to defend the city but other regiments like us from Shanghai being redirected to flee further west to Chungking the wartime capital city.

It was with surprise when Major Chu received a radio message. He told us, 'sorry boys we have reached Wuchang in Wuhan city. But Wuhan is under attack and we have to flee further west to Chungking.'

We arrived at Chungking in April 1939. The land rose sharply in Chungking preventing an attack by river or by land. There are

24

severe bomb raids on the civilians. Slowly I got used to the sirens and bombing raids.

In my office we received hundreds of war materials from the Burma Road. One day I was shocked when a hundred men came and assembled an airplane in two weeks. It was flown away by an old American pilot.

We assembled trucks and armored cars. In a few months I became familiar with Logistics works.

On a bleak Sunday I cycled to work. As I cycled past the Church I saw a figure in the distance. On looking closely I recognized the unforgettable lovely face of Grace Lu coming out of the church. It was a sweet reunion for me and I invited her for dinner.

As I spoke a Japanese plane dropped three bombs which missed the Church by a kilometer.

I complained about the bombings.

'Chungking the wartime capital teased the Japanese Army, too remote in the west for a land attack, and inaccessible to an Army via the river Yangzi as it climbs towards the highest snow mountains near the Himalayas. The Japanese Army dropped three thousand tons of bombs on the city between 1939 and 1941. The most intensive bombing struck us in 1941 the most destructive of all in the Wild West.'

Grace smiled, 'I have been here 16 months and heard that you have been giving talks about war strategy?'

'Ahem yes but only to a small group of army officers. Hey I like to take you out dance and dine. This city is very dull in wartime.'

I dressed neatly and picked her up. She was dressed simply and we went to a hotel dining room where there were soldiers, Americans and businessmen.

'In answer to your question Gary I came to Chungking with Madam Liza Kung as her assistant two years ago. But life for these rich ladies is too unexciting in Chungking. Soon she socialized with the American ladies and one of them offered her a partnership in a Chinatown gold shop in San Francisco. She offered to take me to America but I have aged parents in China. I am

Manageress of her gold shops in Chungking. You? Gary, how did you come to Chungking?'

'Me, I joined the Shanghai Wars in 1937 we lost badly and escaped to Chungking. I am now attached to Logistics, receiving war materials from Burma near Calcutta in India. I dislike the Japanese bombings of civilian targets. Have you seen David Kung lately? Is he in Chungking?'

'David. Well he made many millions as a businessman and his family is connected with the famous banker Kung. He went to America with his mother and Maggie. Poor me I am left alone in Chungking.'

I confess I fell for Grace and we had a splendid evening. We went out together to see the sights around Chungking such as the three Gorges, the stone carvings in Dazu County, the South Hot Spring Park, and Red Crag Memorial Museum.

It was the happiest moment of my life and I was thinking of proposing to her. But it was also the saddest moment of my life when I lost her or really we parted company.

A red rose she came into my life,
Beautify things I see and feel
Then the winds came
The Rose of love blown to other Eden

Grace brightened my life. We spent hours walking along the quiet lanes in the morning, shopping in the Sunday markets and eating the famous Sichuan cuisine. The dark side of Grace's life was in the Black Market. She would take her assistant Miss Lucy Wang and mix with the Auctions. The three gangs were the Kunming Yunnan Gang, the Chungking Sichuan gang and the Guichou Gang. I saw Grace sold gold pieces manufactured in Shanghai and bought diamonds smuggled from Burma. She was a remarkable Manageress yet she did not belong to any gang. They treated her with great respect. Her boss Lisa Kung would remit her millions to buy diamonds and receive millions worth of gold and diamonds.

My interest in Sun Tzu's War ideas remained strong in me. I began to join a small group of war time officers and we discussed the aggressive tactics of the Japanese Army inside China.

I felt excited at linking Sun Tzu's view of War strategy with the two ancient armies of China and Japan. Both are absolute autocratic machines where power rests in the person a Great Warrior of wars. From the mid 1850's to the mid 1940's China tried to modernize to fight off foreign invaders. Similarly Japan through the Japanese Army in China tried to modernize its military hardware and Navy to stop the Russians from grabbing Manchuria. One primary fear of Japanese Army War planners is that if the Russians control Korea or and Manchuria it is a dagger pointed at the heart of Japan. You can say they were obsessed by this fear. But their defensive ambitions grew out of control until they became obsessed with the expansion into China at all costs.

When the Japanese Army Navy defeated the Russians in the Russo Japanese War in 1904 it was a great achievement and pride. That great victory was the beginning of the expansion minded Japanese Army in China. Manchuria is ripe for military conquest. From the need to defend Japan they have moved on to the need to expand in China.

The Expansionary record of the Japanese Army in China or Kwangtung Army can be traced in the following sequence.

1885- Sino Japanese fighting in Korea where Queen Min seeks protection of China. Yuan Shih Kai is defeated. Japan controls Korea.

1894-6—Sino Japanese War. Yuan Shih Kai is defeated. Japan gets concession in Kwangtung Army lease and Shandong, Taiwan and Shanghai concessions.

1900- Boxer War defeat. Burning of Summer Palace Dowager Cixi staged palace coup against young emperor Guang Xu. Installs baby emperor Puyi.

1911 Revolution—Qing Dynasty falls after Marshall Yuan negotiates Pu Yi can reside in Forbidden Palace

1913—Republican Government with Yuan as President

1916- Yuan's promise to hold elections arrives but he expels Sun Yat San to Japan. Song Ji Ren who won majority is assassinated.

1925- Sun Yat San sets up Whampoa military college in south with Russian aid

1925- Sun Yat Sun dies in Beijing temporary ally with Warlord Feng of Shandong and Fengtian clique

1928- Chiang's Northern Expedition takes Nanjing- southern government declared

1928- Jinan Incident- Chiang's advance into Shandong stopped by Japanese Army

1928- Manchurian Incident- Warlord Chang Tso Lin's train explosion assassinated.

1931- Mukden Incident. Japanese Army takes over Mukden Manchuria. Chiang's No Chinese fight back policy a carry over from Yuan Shih Kai days

1932- Jan 28- Shanghai Incident. Chinese 19th Army at Zhabei (Chapei) bordering Wusong attacked, Treaty requires Shanghai International City to be off limit to Chinese Army

1932- Provinces in Manchuria taken over. Manchukuo is proclaimed free from China under Pu Yi ex Emperor of China. Young Marshall son of Chang Tso Lin forced out of Manchuria and Beijing

1936- Xi An Incident Young Marshall kidnaps Chiang but persuades him to sign United Front with Communists

1937- Marco Polo Bridge Incident. Hostilities broke out, marks start of Beiping Tianjin War- Japanese Army drives two fronts from Great Wall north of Beijing and landings at Tianjin to Marco Polo Bridge then west to Beijing. Force the Chinese 29th Army in retreat.

1937- 2nd Sino Japanese War breaks out on two fronts. Shanghai Invasion Expedition at Wusong and Naval Landing at Hang Zhou Bay. Forced March to Nanjing.

1938-1945- 7 years war. Chiang retreats to wartime capital Chungking (Chongging) in Sichuan.

Was there a pattern of planned aggression?

In those early decades Army Dictatorship controls the reporting of military matters by the newspapers. Journalists are careful what they report. Therefore it appears the wars were a series of Incidents which broke out of control.

But as information became more freely available it became clear there was a military war policy of expansion in China.

On the Warlords side it is sensitive to publicly announce the terms of the Sino Japanese treaty which provides for the supervision of the Warlords. Thus we kept wondering why the Warlord of Shandong tolerates Japanese Army Garrisons in the Province. Why the Naval fleet of Japan uses Qingdao as harbor for Japanese ships.

It was only the revelation by western journalists on the Japanese Treaty of 21 Demands secretly signed by Yuan in 1916. It leaked that in 1921 that Treaty was ratified by the western countries at the League of Nations. It caused National shame and demonstrations.

chapter

TWO

2nd Sino Japanese War in 4 Key cities

Memoirs of Lily Shan visit Shanghai

I Lily Shan came to China in the 1997 to meet Mai Lin or Mrs. Ted Tang. I forgot that Ted has a son named Gary. There I was handed Gary's memoirs about the 2nd Sino Japanese War in 1937. Gary's description of people involved in the Nanjing War thrilled me. The KMT Army was inspired by one mission, the hunting down of the Left Wing Army or PLA, encirclement of the headquarters at Yenan to which it had fled in 1937. Why was it such a passionate strategy? Perhaps the words attributed to Chiang the Chief Commander indicate a deeper well of feeling.

'The Japanese Invaders are a disease of the skin, we can wipe it out but the Leftist Army is a disease of the heart.'

I looked for clues in the book Art of War as to why there was such a deep hatred of the Leftist people. One clue is the age or generation of the opposing commanders. Chiang was from a time when China was ruled passionately by the teachings of Confucianism. Respect for the Institutions of Family and worship of our ancestors is a cornerstone. Many gentlemen would declare their respect and love of their mother or father as cornerstone of their life. This implies continuance of the Clan and village culture. The Communists were practicing a foreign thought process which challenged the Confucian village clan and order of life. To the pillars of Confucian life such as Chinese Village and Clan Associations these upstarts who organized mass labor strikes, and seizing of farm lands are incorrigible. The Landlords were horrified and swift to act against these bad rebels.

Perhaps that was what happened when Chiang and the Shanghai Green Gang Boss Due Yueh Sheng or Feng swiftly organized a mass killing of a mass demonstration by workers in a large scale strike in Shanghai. The Leftists called it the Shanghai massacre.

I come to Shanghai to search for the papers of Gary Tang. He is well known as a friend of a Great General and expert on the art of war during the second Sino Japanese war. My newspaper wish to find eye witness accounts of the Sino Japanese war 1937. Who were the Generals and what art in war was important? He wrote about the death of two ancient armies. What did it mean? Tang taught many interested followers to compare Sun Tzu's treatise on war, to the brilliant plans of the Japanese Army in China.

The term class warfare was used by the Leftist Army. They were the Landlord class and we were the Labor or Peasants of the countryside. Chiang organized Encirclement four campaigns to entrap the Leftist Army. He had the service of two brilliant German Generals to conduct the hunt.

This was what I was looking from the writings of Gary Tang but sadly I did not find any mention of their feud. But Gary's writing on the history of the Japanese Kwangtung Army in China was brilliant because it highlights the failures of one man in charge of war that is Yuan Shih Kai. Even in 1885 when he was sent to Korea he took one look at the mean Japanese Ninjas in Seoul at a time when there were no army uniforms he began to avoid a direct fight. He even took leave in Beijing when the Japanese overran Korea. It was a great act of personal survival when Yuan lost the Sino Japanese War 1895 but was able to protect the Empress

Dowager's position as ruler of China. I find Gary Tang's painting of Yuan as the King of Warlord cliques as a fair comment.

In a Shanghai hotel near the Wusong River, I stood up and held the news article closer to my eyes. 'The War of Shanghai 1932 and 1937,' the words stared at me. I had discussed with my friend Professor Wang of Taiwan about the chaotic history which prevailed in China in 1937. The Japanese name the War the Nanjing Incident, the Chinese Army named it the Battle of Nanjing but some historians call it the Second Sino Japanese War.

Professor Wang advised, 'to understand modern China we have to look at the four cultural political movements that played against each other in 1937 inside China. Which of these cultural movements will prevail?

'My father, 'she said, 'was a student leader in the American run University. He took part in the Nationalist Army of Generalissimo Chiang as an army captain. The Nationalist Government won independence in 1911 but the Warlords under Marshall Yuan Shih Kai blocked their founder Sun Yat San from the reins of government. Marshall Yuan Shih Kai pretended that the Imperial Army had joined the Nationalist Revolution. But in truth it was only the military in the western city of Wuhan that mutinied. The Imperial Army headquarters at Beijing, and Nanjing stayed on the sidelines. Yuan manipulated the Republicans pretending to protect the Emperor. He then ushered in the era of Warlords under which the military held the reins of power until his death in 1916. He even tried to crown himself Emperor Hong xian a new emperor but his regional commanders objected. He abdicated and a few months later died of uremia. Yuan as a military leader was weak in the arts of war. His opponent the Japanese Army in China viewed him as weak with no will to fight them openly. But as the head of government at Beijing he would honor the treaties which he signed. Inside China he was most powerful.

Warlords from 1913 to 1928 symbolize the dying Confucian Landlord culture. The Warlords are obedient to their rulers whether it is to the Manchu emperors or Japanese Army in China as victors of the First Sino Japanese War. Yuan Shih Kai symbolized the Confucian gentry holding absolute power in North China. He was defeated in 1884 in Korea and in China in 1894 when the Chinese Navy of Admiral Teng was destroyed at Wei Hai Wei and pig tail Admiral Teng committed suicide. By paying huge money and territory concessions to Japan he preserved the rule of the Dowager Cixi who died in 1908. After her he became absolute ruler in Beijing and Warlord of warlords. The Japanese Army preferred other smaller Warlords to weaken the power of Yuan. Thus they recognized Chang Tso Lin as Warlord in Manchuria. His independence from Yuan and China was demonstrated when on two occasions Yuan transferred him to be Governor in Mongolia. He simply ignored the request.

I find Chang Tso Lin or Zhang Zuo Lin one of the pillars of Chinese military power in Manchuria between 1904 and 1928. He started as a mountain bandit. His band expanded in a big way when he helped the Japanese Army in the Russo Japanese War 1904. He was friendly with Japanese Army and helped them grab control over the South Manchurian Railway which was built by the Russians. With Japanese support Yuan was steered into the action of confirming him as the Inspector of the Army and later Governor of Manchuria. In return he was one of a few Warlords who supported Yuan's attempt to be Emperor Hong xian in February 1916. When Yuan died in September 1916 Warlord Chang gained control of all Manchuria and fought to control Beijing against Duan Ji Rui of the Anhui clique. The Japanese Army in Kwangtung had expanded from 14000 men but their real power was far greater than their numbers. They valued the South Manchurian Railway but by 1928 they blew up Chang's train. With Chang's son later driven out of Manchuria in 1932 the Japanese set up the new state of Manchukuo in 1932 under Emperor Pu Yi.

The Japanese Kwangtung Army in the early 1930's underwent a radical transition when militarism (military rules over civilian government), ultra nationalistic ambitions (nationalism beyond Japanese shores) and fascism (tyranny and oppression) began to take hold of the middle ranking officers. These military officers belonged to many secret societies which influenced the cabinet. War Ministers Navy and Army Ministers are elected by the military. Without a War Minister the civilian cabinet has to resign.

The ultra Nationalist societies, secretly, within the military was critical of the civilian Prime Ministers which seemed to restrict military expansion into China. The civilian cabinet was friendly to the newly established 1928 government of Chiang Kai Shek at Nanjing whose party the KMT (Kuo Min Tang or Nationalist Party) threatened to grab control of government at Beijing.

To the ultra secret societies of middle officers within the Japanese Army in China Manchuria was won with blood in the bloody Russo Japanese War in 1904. It was unthinkable that the civilian cabinet would recognize the KMT government and indirectly agree to abrogation of the Sino Japanese War Treaty of 1896 which leased Manchuria to Japan. The word leased was unsatisfactory because it made the Army humiliated as tenants of Manchuria when the situation in reality was that they were the over lords of that bountiful country. Even the Chinese over lord Warlord Chang has to walk carefully on Manchurian Colonial soil. The power of the Japanese Army in China was restrained and reined in by the civilian Cabinet. But the ultra secret societies believed that War is not a problem and were confident of militarism as the solution.

To the serving Japanese officers as they discussed matters in their secret societies they felt that to lose a battle for Manchuria on a piece of paper when they were all that much stronger militarily angers the Gods of War.

To them China is not a united country as claimed by Chiang as they have witnessed a hundred Warlords scheming against each other and fighting for Japanese patronage. This endemic infighting for power is a bad example for the proud officers of Japan who are united by love of their country, pride in the unity between Army and Navy and distrust of the Chinese Warlords who shifts loyalty and betray their own countrymen. At this time the Chinese Warlords are divided into three cliques, the Fengtian (Mukden) clique, the Chih Li clique (Beijing Hebei) and the Anhui clique (Shanghai, Shandong and Nanjing). When the Fengtian clique of Chang Tso Lin in Manchuria lost the battle against Anhui clique of Duan Ji Rui, in 1928 he sought to return back to his old headquarters at Fengtian (Mukden). But the Japanese preferred a weak puppet such as his deputy a General Yang Yu Ting rather than have Chang as Warlord whose 300000 men army is sure to cause a struggle for power. Chang's private train was blown up in 1928 as it reached Mukden. It also signaled a change in Japanese war policy in Manchuria and possibly in the readiness to tame the growing might of Chiang's Army.

Chiang after all is merely another Warlord.

Japanese Prime Minister. Inukai, Tsuyoshi was shot in 1932 and as he pleaded to speak, the league of blood officers said, 'Dialogue is useless.' Militarism would be the means to an end. This militarism saw the push to make Manchukuo a puppet state. The civilian government's role in international obligations was brushed aside. And the complaint was strong against the Washington Treaty on Naval parity ratio of 5:3:3 and soon unilaterally scrapped.

The Cabinet became dominated by the military. Against this background I realize the War preparations by the Japanese Army in China against four key cities namely Beijing, Tianjin, Shanghai and Nanjing which escalated into the Second Sino Japanese Wars was part of a grand scheme, the military conquest of China.

In the provinces of Henan, Hebei and Chahar other Warlords were recognized by Japan. Yuan's peace treaty concessions to Japan include key Provinces such as Manchuria, Shandong, Taiwan and small concessions in Tianjin, and Shanghai. Key Warlords in Hebei, Chahar, and Rehe paid more homage to Japan than Yuan in Beijing. The Warlord Yuan's brand of military lordship was corrupt and a sad period of national weakness in history.

I looked on the Chinese and Japanese military as descendants of ancient armies where the War lords have personal power and absolute power over the military. It was the dream of Japanese Samurai Lords to conquer China. Somehow in 1937 they faced the taunts and call of All China Chinese demonstrators to drive them out of Manchuria where they have set up Manchukuo a puppet state. In the ranks of Japanese ultra Nationalist middle officers the reaction was to abandon the old signed peace treaties, resume the old wars and punish the anti Japanese armies of Nationalist governments. The military at least in the 1930's dominated the political climate after a Prime Minister and 3 Ministers had been assassinated in Tokyo.

'Osaka Shimbun newspaper on May 15 1932 reported that a Prime Minister Inukai and three Ministers were assassinated by 11 Navy cadets who called themselves inspired by the League of Blood. The League of Blood has a leader Nissho Inoue who advocates military revival by killing political and business leaders and Ministers who blindly obey the western imperial countries. The Washington Conference reduced Japan's Navy parity to third rank.'

As a friend Professor Wang added.

'At their trial a petition containing 350000 signatures was tendered plus a letter pleading for leniency from 11 youths from Niigata who asked to be executed instead. Eleven bloodied fingers were included as a sign of good faith. The cadets received two years or less. In my view the Young Turk Colonels in Manchuria China may realize they have to fight America and Russia later. It does not take a smart army chief to realize that to fight America and Russia you will need land in China, people labor and modern weapons.'

When Nazi Germany rise as a big power in Europe the militarists in Japan somehow justified the view whether right or wrong the winning of a war is the prime consideration. They were buoyed by the fact that they had captured Beijing and Tianjin and are in a position to set up a government to run China.

I responded, 'No Wang it was the Feng Shui of 1937. It saw the enormous power of Nazi Germany so powerful that by 1941 the Empire of France had been conquered and French Indo China had been given to them as a gift. The mighty British was on the edge of defeat confined in Britain with the Battle of Britain bombings of London. Hitler is unstoppable because of his Panzers.

Then in September that year the Secretary of State gave an ultimatum to them they must clear out of French Indochina as well as China. Yes Feng Shui masters advised them that going to war were a wise move.'

Back in China, the Nationalist Army swept the Warlords in Nanjing from power, in 1928. They marched north against the

Warlord government in Beijing which was under Chang Tso Lin shakily under pressure.

In Japan from April 1927 to 1929 the Prime Minister was G Tanaka a former General. He was under pressure because in Nanjing 1928 while Chiang's Northern Expedition attacked the Warlords Sun Chuan Fang many Japanese were killed or injured. Relations were tense when Tanaka sent a 4000 men force into Japanese leased territory at Jinan to protect Japanese civilians. This was at the time labeled by the press as the First Shandong Expedition.

Somewhere somehow the former General G Tanaka of an older generation of soldiers and the new generation of active officers in the Kwangtung Army may have had a difference of views on Wars in China. Tanaka was involved in the First Sino Japanese War 1894 and some believed he drafted some of the Treaty. Tanaka was accused by the Chinese as having authored the Tanaka Memorial which advocates the takeover of China by military wars. This was denied. But it is believed that this was the view of a few of the secret societies rather than Tanaka who as an older generation General was out of touch with contemporary militarists. He was also very angry at the assassination of Chang Tso Lin calling for prosecution of the perpetrators. But Tanaka was now a civilian elder statesman prime minister and the military did not act on his suggestions. But the statements attributed to Chang Tso Lin that he might join the Army of Chiang, was the final blow. Mutiny on the Kwangtung plains is in the air when a Warlord changes sides even though it is a mere rumor the counter attack is swift and deadly, Chang's train is blown up.

Tanaka sent in the 4000 soldiers to Jinan as the First Shandong Expedition. Was this a peace keeping force? Yes for a time there was peace but suddenly the machinations of Warlord clique's turns into motion. Against the orders of Tokyo, a General Fukuda of the Tianjin Garrison sends in 8000 soldiers along the strategic Jiaoyi railway to Jinan. The press hails this as the Second Shandong Expedition. On the Chinese side Warlord Zhang ZongChang Chang Tso Lin's man evacuates from Jinan but General He Yaozu moves into Jinan. The play for war had begun which would not end until the Second Sino Japanese War ends with the fall of Shanghai then Nanjing.

A skirmish occurred when 12 Japanese were killed but the Japanese conducted a public autopsy showing that a Japanese man had been castrated. Japanese sent in more men. Chiang sent in a negotiator Cai Gongshi with 16 men to negotiate. This did not get a response but they were kept prisoner. When this negotiator requested the General to pass on his suggestions upwards to his superiors in Tokyo and the contents released to the public what did he get?

Well his feet was broken, his teeth smashed, his tongue cut and he was taken to the street and shot dead. The Japanese attacked and drove off the Chinese Division with 15000 civilian casualties. Chiang's attempt to advance the Northern Expedition from Nanjing to Beijing was stopped in its track at Jinan. Tanaka resigned en mass in July 1929 realizing he was not an insider. A proposal to appoint him a Field Marshall was cancelled due to a controversy about some payments.

The Incident established two facts. One Chiang's progress from Nanjing to Beijing is difficult instead he had to worry about a military counter attack which would blow out into a Second Sino Japanese War. Secondly, the period of reliance on Warlords to rule as surrogate rulers has been discarded in favor of militarism, whatever military conquers military gets to keep.

Chiang was confronted by the formidable and well organized Japan Army inside China. In the Jinan Incident of 1928 the Nationalists unwisely sent a head of deputation to negotiate. The solders broke his leg, smashed his teeth, cut his tongue, and shot him and 16 other members of his Deputation. In its extreme form the imperialist mentality tolerates no disrespect from the Warlord troops nor Nationalist Army branded together. They were ordered not to approach Jinan within 20 km of the city but broke the warning. Indiscipline was a serious issue and punishment is swift and severe.

They did not know how to deal with the Japanese Army in Kwantung Manchuria. Their army was mainly infantry. Confucian culture of the Nationalist government is less despotic than the Warlords but it was not a warlike culture. In 1937 the Nationalist Army was patriotic but untested in battle.

The Japanese Army in China came through hard fought wars namely the Sino Japanese War 1894, the 1898 Boxer War and the 1904 Russo Japanese War. The culture of the Japan army inside China is military expansion and is known for its War Code for which indiscipline is a serious offence. In 1937 rapid changes in the world took place whereby western imperialism is being questioned by westerners themselves. However the Japanese Army and Nazi Germany held strong views on imperialism in particular the right to rule of a powerful country over a weak country. In 1937 they faced the decision whether go to war with the Nationalist Army of China based at Nanjing. They decided on War in August 1937 when the idea and propaganda of a one million Invasion Army to capture Nanjing was deployed into action. This refutes the Chinese Generals who later promoted the fiction that it was an Incidental War.

The fourth political cultural Movement in China was the Leftist Communist Army. In 1937 they were the smallest army in China numbering 20000 having no big guns artillery or planes but mainly an infantry type guerrilla army. In 1935 Chiang Kai Shek encircled their army in Kwangsi forcing it to escape via the 12500 km over 13 months Long March to Yenan in the North West. The ideal society in China had long been a Confucian gentry and Confucian Landlord society close to the Land. The Leftist Army which later grew into the PLA is close to the Land but from the downtrodden Peasantry's side. Thus it was class warfare. Peasants are peasants born to be ruled.

Alienated from the Gentry culture the leaders sought to replace the Gentry's stranglehold on Land by abolishing the Land ownership system. This created deep seated great enmity with the Nationalist Army. The leftists adopted the Russian model in 1937 with a modified new homegrown model based on Peasant Rebellion and Anti class Corruption. They targeted bad landlords and bad practices at village level. This anti landlord corruption movement gained wide acceptance as against the Nationalist officials who were great landlords themselves. But in 1937 they were too weak as an army confined to the remote North West.

The first battle was between the Nationalist against the Japanese Army in China in July 1937. It was called the Beijing Tianjin wars followed by the August 1937 Second Sino Japanese war against Shanghai and Nanjing.

To the Japanese war planners at Garrison Kwantung in Manchuria the conquest of China must begin with good plans. The conquest of Beijing the traditional capital of the Emperors now left without a head of government was very well planned with 20000 soldiers from the Great Wall zone attacking eastwards to Beijing. This is supported by a sea landing at Tianjin advancing westwards towards Beijing against the defenders the 29th army. Simultaneously in the south a million men army to land at Shanghai and Hang Zhou Bay followed by a scorched earth advance towards Nanjing in the mid west. Furthermore this war like policy held by Army ultra Nationalist officers inside China, cannot be carried out openly but silently even secretly within the army because the civilian Prime Ministers in Tokyo hold on to a policy of recognizing the Chinese governments.

On the Manchurian side, the 1928 assassination of Marshall Chang Tso Lin was an orchestrated attempt by the Deputy Commander in Chief named General Yang Yuting to convene a Council meeting to vote himself the new Commander in preference to the late Marshall's son. Being over confident he had voiced the opinion that the Young Marshall is not fit to succeed the old man. The young Marshall in his youth was a womanizer, opium addict who cured himself and pleasure seeker in Shanghai town but now reformed. The Young Marshall Chang Xue Liang was away in China at the time of the assassination. He was unable to attend in Mukden. However the old guard General Chang Xuoxiang proved loyal to his late friend's son as successor and delayed the Council vote. Seen as a protégé of the Japanese Yang Yuting had a strong private army and held an exhibition where Chang's son, his boss in theory was invited as a mere ordinary delegate. Further General Yang demanded that he be given the power of veto over executive Council appointments. The last straw came when he brought his nominee to the palatial Mansion cum Headquarters of Chang Xue Liang. He demanded his Deputy be appointed to the post of Commissioner of the South Manchuria Railways a powerful position. Today the tourists to Mukden (now Shenyang) are shown the 40 room Mansion which was the headquarters of Chang Xue Liang in 1929. The young Marshall realized that Yang Yuting was somehow implicated in the assassination of his late father, and grabbing for power. In that large room called the Tiger Room he asked for time to consider then ordered the Security Chief to have Yang and his Deputy shot for treason. He allied himself with Chiang's Nanjing government but slowly came under military pressure from the Japanese Army as military actions started in the Great Wall Provinces such as Chahar, Rehe, and Jehol and even in Mukden his late father's capital. By 1937 Chiang had only one army inherited from the Chang Xue Liang that was defending Beijing. Xue Liang himself had become Chiang's palace prisoner, after the Xi An incident. The Japanese Army was planning military moves to drive his 29th Army out of Beijing.

'He was not a genius at military battle a far cry from his father Chang Tso Lin.' I remarked.

Professor Wang raised her voice.

'No but Marshall Chang Xue Liang's refusal to imitate the great stooge Yuan Shih Kai to act as a puppet ruler, in 1936 inspired millions of young Chinese men and women to join the military to fight the Japanese Army in China. They gave their lives in sacrifice for their country. My grandfather did that and died in the Battle of Shanghai. That is what this poor bullied patriot son of a Warlord did for his country.'

'Well he died rich in Hawaii did he not?'

'No as at 1997 he is alive in Hawaii. Let us get back to 1937. China was weak with a weak army. Japan won the Battles of Beijing, Tianjin, Shanghai and Nanjing, but the patriotic love of their country inspired millions to join the Nationalist army and also the Leftist Armies. The War Machine of Japan could not control such a large rebellion. The seeds of patriotic people were ignited inspired by such brave acts of a young helpless Manchurian commander in chief. Yes time had changed the art of war and no matter however quick they built their war machine millions of Chinese joined their army in answer to the call for new fighters.'

'I cannot argue as I was not there in those days. I accept your views.'

Truth is a kin to fiction. The veil of Japanese de facto rule over Chinese stooge Yuan Shih Kai was necessary in 1904 to avoid western interference. China was labeled as the sick man of Asia with relatives fighting for her wealth. The USA tried to promote the

Monroe Doctrine to assure that no single foreign country gets exclusive rights. When the Japanese won the Russo Japanese War, western countries intervened and forced the return of Port Arthur to China. But by 1931 the western military presence in Manchuria was almost absent. The Manchurian army was disunited with a pro Japanese faction. The time for takeover of the four disunited Manchurian Provinces seemed to have become ripe.

It was a slow process. For many years from 1896 to 1928 the Japanese Army preferred to stay in the background. The Warlords become notorious Japanese front rulers.

When the Warlord Chang Tso Lin was blown up in his personal train in 1928 it signified that the Japanese Army presence in Manchuria is changing from passive invasion, to military takeover. The military capture of Beijing the Northern Capital became an achievable objective and Tianjin the seaport approach in the north had already been garrisoned in the foreign concessions.

In 1931 in the 9/18 Mukden Incident, the railway track was blown up and Japanese Army started military attacks which confined the Chinese troops to their quarters who then retreated to Beijing. In fact after the 1928 Manchurian Incident where Marshall Chang's train blew up, the main Manchurian Army had quietly withdrawn into China. It was a mere formality for the Japanese to takeover all of Manchuria. This they did and in 1932 the new Empire of Manchukuo under Henry Pu Yi was promulgated. The ceding of Manchukuo caused many protests from Chinese politicians and the public.

In 1936 Manchuria now known as the North Eastern Army in Shansi under General Chang Xue Liang forced Chiang Kai Shek who was kidnapped to declare a United Front against Japan known as the Xi An Incident. What was Japan's response? Japan's response was to plan military action against the North Eastern Army of Chang Xue Liang at Beijing and the new Republican Army of Chiang Kai Shek based at Nanjing.

By 1937 the Marco Polo Bridge Incident of 7/7 37 erupted. A lost Japanese soldier was reported. Japan sought permission to enter the Chinese city of Wanping for a search. Wanping next to the river Yong Ding was a very small walled city. When the request was refused an attack was mounted driving the Chinese soldiers from the area. After bombardments by artillery

42

and planes the Japanese Army requested the 29th Division to retreat past the River Yongding to the south. Again a refusal resulted in prolonged bombing and artillery attacks. The Chinese radioed for reinforcements and supplies from Chiang Kai Shek in Nanjing but it became clear that Chiang was unable to send reinforcements as promised because he was under threat of a million men army invasion landing at Shanghai. A second front was directed at Hangzhou Bay near the Suzhou lines.

On 18 August 1937 General Kawabe entered Beijing and declared him self to be Governor of Beijing. With a force of 20000 men he had driven the 46000 men 29th Army out of Beijing. Many regiments were destroyed by Japanese Air bombardment, Big gun artillery and armored cars. The remaining Chinese infantry then were attacked heavily. At Tianjin General Zhang zhi zhong, was allowed to remain Mayor but without a soldier under him he secretly left for Nanjing. General Sung faced plane and artillery bombardment and retreated to Shandong where the Chinese Warlord Han Fu Qu refused his decimated army from crossing the Hwang Ho (Yellow) River. Sung was forced to downsize his remaining men of 8000 after a battle in Hebei into guerrilla units retreating towards Sichuan as Nanjing was under attack.

Attack on Shanghai and Hang Zhou Bay.

From the newspaper articles which Professor Wang lent me I retraced the attack at Shanghai and Su Zhou via Hang Zhou Bay. Simultaneously a massive naval marine invasion force from troops and ships and planes originating from Japanese Bases in Japan, Shandong and Taiwan is to land at the Bay of Hangzhou to wipe out defensive Chinese army forces in Chinese sectors of Shanghai. A push towards Nanjing capital of the southern government of Chiang Kai Shek is the central objective.

Tianjin had always had a Japanese presence since the 1894 Sino Japanese War over Korea and the 1898 Boxer War over protection of foreign citizens from chaotic armed rebels. The late Warlord's son Marshall Chang Xue Liang ruled Beijing in name but his North eastern Army has retreated safely from Manchuria and Beijing to the near western Province of Shansi between Beijing and Xian. One big Division remains near Beijing the Chinese 29th Route Army. The military threat from the Japanese Kwantung Army in Manchuria can be traced back to the time when the late Marshall Chang Tso Lin in 1928 sought to travel back to Manchuria from Beijing after suffering reverses against the Warlord cliques of Chih Li and Chiang in the Central Plains War.

Why did he rush back to Mukden in a hurry? Marshall Chang Tso Lin has a retinue of old Generals and internal affairs spies watching his power base back in Mukden. Old Marshall Chang's relations with Japan's army in China had undergone a fundamental change when a new Commander of the Kwangtung army garrison took charge. Perhaps he suspected his second in command Yang Yuting with a potential plot. With the rise of Chiang's new Republican Army, the 1928 Jinan Incident and the 1932 Shanghai Incident the possibility of Chiang taking over the Chinese government in Beijing is faced squarely by the Japanese Kwantung Army. The Nationalist supporters of Chiang's government had proclaimed that the Japanese sponsored Kingdom of Manchukuo newly formed in 1932 under former Chinese Emperor Pu Yi is part of China. This was supported by the League of Nation's Lytton Commission but the Japanese resigned from the League when pressed.

From 1928 to 1937 is Japan ready to go to War with China again?

The answer is yes, if the territorial gains won after the Sino Japanese War in 1894 and Russo Japanese War in 1904 is to be preserved and not to be lost the Kwangtung Garrison has a sacred duty to protect Japan's gains in China. This theme held the imaginations of a generation of ultra Nationalist serving officers in Manchuria. Some of these officers were idealistic calling for the liberation of China (from the west or from the greedy corrupt officials and big business monopolies.) Although the Japanese Army is influenced by many ultra Nationalist middle rank officers in secret societies, the civilian government in Tokyo was a restraining factor on the war minded middle officers. However by 1926 the public mutiny in Tokyo and assassinations of a Prime Minister in Tokyo had given the war minded factions in Manchuria the upper hand against Chiang Kai Shek as the strong man of China. In later years several of these idealistic officers became Generals and key commanders in World War 2. There were reports during the 1945 War Crimes trials that the Japanese Chief Commander of the Shanghai Invasion column was a good friend of Chiang Kai Shek in the early days. But when ordered as one of two former Commanders and Governors of Taiwan to head the 1937 Invasion force he remarked, 'Chiang Kai Shek has to be defeated convincingly.' Alternatively a second report quoted him as saying, 'There's no solution except to break the power of Chiang Kai-shek by capturing Nanking. That is what I must do.'

History records that he was hanged for war crimes in the Nanjing War Massacres after his convictions. Was he a ruthless War General who presided over the Nanjing massacre?

Historians blamed the Nanjing Expeditionary Commander at his trial and he Iwame Matsu accepted responsibility though other historians held he was a scapegoat. The truth lies somewhere in between for he was known to have helped built a statue of Buddhist Goddess of Mercy and faced in the direction of Nanjing. But his record also shows that he was a veteran of the 1904 Russo Japanese War and close associate of more military minded colleagues and ultra nationalist secret societies. He accepted responsibility for the wild Nanjing massacre and paid with a capital conviction. Such is the code of the military strategy.

The only claimant to the Chinese government in 1937 is Chiang Kai Shek whose newly founded army is confined to the inland city of Nanjing 600 miles west of seaboard Shanghai. The Japanese Army garrisoned in China in 1937 numbered about 30000 in Manchuria with a similar number at the ready based in Korea and bases in Taiwan. It played a major part in guarding Japanese interests in Manchuria, Hebei (which surrounds Beijing), Shandong, Shanghai, and Taiwan.

I took a deep breath when I realized that the Japanese Army in China in 1937 was a formidable match against the puny armies of Warlords including Chiang's Revolutionary army. The only other Foreign Army inside China was the Fourth Marines Regiment of USA which had about 1 to 2000 Marines at the Base at Soochow Creek in Shanghai and a further 500 Marines based at Tianjin.

Figure 6: Marines of Soochow Creek march to their
Internment 1941
Source:www.usmcpresentarms.com/adsusmc_china_sooch-
ow...

By the standards of 1937 the numerical size of the Japanese Army in China is large compared to the small Warlord armies. They have ample reserves in Korea, Formosa (Taiwan) and home land. Their Naval and air power in 1937 was among the world's best.

Figure 7: Marshall Chang Tso Lin's train blown up in Manchuria:
Source; Wikipedia

I paused from my research of the old wars. In the fading light of the hotel room's balcony I looked down at the Wusong River flowing gently down towards the Shanghai Bridge (Bai-dahoqiao) where the smaller River joins up with the Huangpu (Whangpoo) River of Shanghai. It was not named Wusong River in the 1920's but the Americans called it Soo Chow Creek and for those who remembered the old vibrant 1920's Shanghai an American Marine Base of 2000 was a prominent feature of So-ochow Creek.

Figure 8: Soo Chow Creek (Wusong river) Source:Wikipedia

If I was back in time in 1937 I would have witnessed the dying days of the Colonial International Treaty city of Shanghai under which the rule of Britain, America and France was to be shot to ashes by the 1937 Wars of Shanghai and Nanjing. I looked at the picture of the Marines being marched to their Internment Camp.

The newly founded 1928 Republic of China under General Chiang Kai Shek had a half million army on paper and when in January 28 1932 one of his zealous commander of the tenth army moved a division of 20000 soldiers to Chapei or Zhapei close to the International city of Shanghai only the Japanese Army had the numbers to drive them out of Treaty Shanghai. At the Japanese sector of Wusong in Shanghai four Japanese monks of a Buddhist sect were killed in Chinese riots and arson. The Japanese Amy inside China was quick alert and ready for a local showdown. The fighting was quick, brief but without mass air and artillery support the Japanese lost 10000 soldiers. In peace negotiations the Chinese 10th Division was sent south to Fujien. As part of the peace treaty China was forbidden to station armed soldiers in International Shanghai only light armed policemen or security officers were permitted. It is a breach of Treaty for Chinese soldiers to enter Shanghai a Treaty Port. In the past regimes of Warlord Yuan Shih Kai and Wu Pei Fuh when Shanghai was ruled by Chinese Warlords the Warlord Army was careful not to send soldiers into the International Treaty Port. The foreign countries were victors of the 1896 Sino Japanese War Treaty and 1900 Boxer War Treaty under which peace was granted on condition China does not send armed soldiers to disturb the peaceful occupation of leased territories. China had to pay war reparations but no cash was outlaid in exchange the British set up a Chinese customs from which revenue is offset. Japan after the First World War in 1918 took over the German possessions in China such as Taiwan, Shandong, Qingdao and Wei Hai Wei (including foreign concessions inside Tianjin). This transfer of sovereignty to Japan was affirmed when Warlord Yuan Shih Kai was forced to sign the Treaty of 21 Demands in 1916 the year he died. His successor Warlord Duan Jirui ratified it in 1921 amidst country wide mass demonstrations which led to the founding of the left wing May 4th Movement. These treaties were never made public by Yuan.

Japan had the most to lose if the Chiang Kai Shek government abandoned or disowned these Treaties. Military action slowly became a necessary option or response. The small American establishment in Tianjin of 500 Marines was a mere spectator staffed by officers who later became famous such as MacArthur.

In 1928 one of Chiang Kai Shek's divisions entered the province of Shandong but the Japanese Army warned them off with a military Incident called the Jinan Incident in which the Chinese negotiator had his tongue, cut off. Hands off the Chinese territories given up by Yuan Shih Kai by way of signed military treaties. These treaties include the 1896 Sino Japanese War Treaty, 1904 Russo Japanese War and 1898-1900 Boxer War Treaty. It caused extreme concern to the military planners of the Japanese Army inside China based at Kwantung Manchuria when the new Chinese government does not obey the Treaty Terms as their old governments did. Their problem was that if the newly established 1928 Republican Government of China wishes to dishonor these Treaties then as Victor in those old war treaties they may resume the hostilities even grab new territories. To add insult to the dishonoring of former war treaties the Chinese protestors had called for a national boycott of Japanese Goods and organized country wide demonstrations against Japanese Army inside China. An unwritten law in the tradition of ancient wars is that the warriors may punish even kill if captured cities behave disrespectfully towards the victors. We must not forget that in 1928 at the same moment that Chiang's Northern Expedition conquered the Warlord vassals of Japan at Nanjing, the Japanese Army staged an explosion on the train of the last Warlord Chang Tso Lin of Manchuria paving the way for control of the whole of Manchuria three years later in 1931. The Incident of Mukden in 1931 was an excuse for an attack and occupation of All Manchuria at the expense of the Warlord Chang Tso Lin's son. Then in 1932 the same thing happened and the border Provinces were taken over as the cover for Henry Pu Yi to be crowned as the Emperor of Manchuria in 1932. Manchuria was safely in the hands of Japan until 1945. The League of Nations condemned the action saying that Manchuria is Chinese land. The Lytton Commission's findings were ignored.

From 1932 we go forward to 1937 when the Japanese Army in China organized attacks called the Marco Polo Bridge Incident of 7/7/1937. It escalates into a takeover of China's Northern Capital at Beijing and the Seaport of Tianjin with its nearby naval Port of Wei Hai Wei. The same battle planners in August 1937 launched the million men army in the south aimed at Chinese held Shanghai and the strong Su Zhou line of forts. One column of half million men attacked Shanghai via the Battle of Shanghai in August 1937 then marched and advanced along the River towns towards Nanjing which they reached by November 1937. A second column of half a million men landed on Hangzhou Bay and attacked Suzhou and then force marched a line of inland cities towards Nanjing the capital of Chiang Kai Shek. The overall target was Chiang Kai Shek and the aim to defeat him completely as a Chinese leader as well as deny him the capacity to send reinforcements to his besieged Generals in the North especially General Sung of the 29th route Army. Fifty years in the past in the 1894 Sino Japanese war the Chinese loser Viceroy Yuan Shih Kai signed away valuable concessions to the Japanese victors and remained in power obeying the Treaty terms. Perhaps Chiang may accept military reality.

But by 1937 the old Confucian world has vanished and took the Japanese Army by surprise. After conquering Nanjing, they founded a puppet government and a Chinese leader named Wang Jing Wei as a puppet Chinese Prime Minister but millions of young rebels joined the other side. Wang Jing Wei was the Deputy of Sun Yat San when the latter died in Beijing in 1925 in the shelter of his supposed Ally Warlord Feng Yu Xiang who betrayed his ally Wu Pei Fuh of the Chih Li clique and took over Beijing the capital for a short while. He fought Chiang in the succession dispute and lost in 1926. When Sun was in danger from a Warlord of Guangdong named Chen Jiong Ming Chiang in 1922 saved him thus moving in as Sun's successor.

Chiang's defiant fighting against the Japanese Army in China gathered support.

To their amazement they (the Japanese) witnessed the old Chiang Kai Shek army having been defeated rose again and again with new divisions equipped with tanks by their western allies especially America. New battles were re fought in the North, south and west of China and a 3 million Japanese army was tied down in China for 8 years till 1945. For example Suzhou were taken, retaken and taken again. In the Battle of Taierchuang near Su Zhou they suffered a big reverse.

> One of the many war poems went like this,
> The clash of two military traditions,
> Confucian soldiery against the Samurai
> Military China divided by North and South
> Military Japan united by ultra Nationalist zeal
> China's program a million infantry
> Japan's of tanks, planes, ships
> motorized columns and artillery

These points summarized the rush to adopt western armies and technology.

Chinese military leaders tried to westernize but the choice (made by Empress Cixi) of Yuan Shih Kai as army Viceroy was a failure.

Japanese leaders such as Yamagata and Count Ito westernized the Japanese Army into the best fighting force in Asia.

The Japanese Army inside China became a powerful force.

In the 1880's Chinese leaders such as Zhang zitong and Li Hung Chang tried to start the western style army but their eventual army with graduates from the Baoding military college under principal Yuan Shih Kai, were defeated in wars against Japan.

The Japanese military structure was dominated by former Samurai leaders in the 1890's such as Yamagata. He tried to westernize their military and improve quality of their officers to produce a highly trained Corp of Army and Navy officers comparable to the west. It was the Prussian model he chose. They produced a fighting force with good military skills and morale. This was supported by state of the art Naval ships, tanks, air planes, bombers and artillery. Unfortunately I observed their main and primary target was the liberation of China my country and use of its vast resources. I am fascinated but lost in the number of published materials on the wars of 1937. From competition with the Russians in Manchuria they gained territories inside China in Shandong, Taiwan, the Ryuku Islands, and Shanghai Wusong. Many Warlords found it profitable to be close to the Japan Army in China rather than with Yuan Shih Kai.

'Lily you are lost in a dream,' my boyfriend David Pang spoke softly in my ears. I was absorbed with the old wars. There was eyewitness accounts of the Sihang Warehouse where 400 Chinese soldiers staged a fight to the last man being bombed and attacked till only a few left. The western onlookers and officials pleaded for them to be allowed to escape.

'Sorry to interrupt you Lily but we and the American Chinese Brotherhood are desperately short of time. We must find the Lost Figurine of a Unicorn before the Hong Kong Chinese Mafia does. It helps us to be free from their control. To help you I have brought over from Taiwan the good Professor Wang.'

David's face is tired as he trudged the room waiting while I read the Memoirs for vital clues of the 1937 wars. I liked to read slowly and sometimes digress far from the vital search for clues. David was worried that this was one such, time as the smile on my face showed. I was reaching far back in time trying to relive the bad days of the 1937 wars of Shanghai and Nanjing.

Professor Wang brushed her spectacles.

'Yes Lily I am personally interested in the Sino Japanese Wars because they originated from Japanese traditions about invasion from Korea and Manchuria in the Mongol Dynasty.'

Secret societies are used to help in gathering information. The Japanese Army has the Kempeitei to perform this task.

The Chinese secret societies developed during the times of Coxinga. Coxinga of Taiwan known by his Ming Dynasty title Lord of Surnames, Kuo Xing Ye. His Rebellion against the Qing Dynasty was centered in the coasts of Fujien Province for 20 years until they forced him to flee to Taiwan. He drove out the small Dutch Colony of Zeelandia. Secret codes and secret membership of triad societies were vital to survive the Qing secret police force and today the secretive triads survive and thrive as Global criminal gangs.

'No no Professor Wang, excuse me I have digressed. II am reading an equally fascinating 1937 Special Report written by Gary Tang as special secret emissary of his good friend General Kar Sher. It has great historical value I think.'

'Tell me more.'

'Well, Sino Japanese War of 1937 at Beijing, Tianjin, Shanghai and Nanjing!' the words spitted from my mouth as I trembled at the atrocities of the Japanese soldiery as they force marched their destructive Army to capture Nanjing. Their invasion force's twin assault columns of a million men army swept through Shanghai and headed towards Nanjing where the Chinese southern capital lie waiting. If Nanjing falls All of China is theirs something dreamed of by the ancient military of Japan Lords of Japan. The war columns marched using a scorched earth approach towards the fortress city of Nanjing. It is the symbolic capital of China. Their military goal was to strongly and soundly defeat Chiang Kai Shek and his newly founded National army. If Chiang Kai Shek can be defeated all China is theirs.

What about the west? America has always had a close relationship with the Soong Family and one of its daughters is Mrs. Chiang Kai Shek. Did the Japanese Army factor in this possibility that in the long term the western countries will intervene? This is a gross miscalculation to think only of 1937? But America had just got out of the 1929 Wall Street Crash and economic depression. Britain has its hands full with Nazi Germany.

Will America intervene to assist China?

The first answer is that yes it is a miscalculation by the Japanese Army inside China to think only of 1937 politics. But they faced tremendous pressure from home politics when in 1932 Inukai the old Japanese Prime Minister was assassinated. In 1936 a mutiny by young cadets was put down. The new PM Konoe tried to send a negotiator to Chiang but the negotiator was detained. In short the threats by young Chinese demonstrators for Japan to get out of Manchuria provoked their military pride. Time has changed.

The answer is yes to the American involvement but quietly and not openly in 1932. Russia has had problems with the Japanese Army in Mongolia resulting in a tank warfare victory at Nomonhan. Yes in 1939 the Russian General Zhukov in Mongolia deployed 498 tanks without infantry to destroy a 30000 Japanese Army at Nomonhan near Khalkin Ghoi. Then in September 1941 America demanded that Japan get out of China and French Indo China and four countries ABCD America Britain Canada and Dutch imposed oil and total trade embargo on Japan.

Japan faced two choices, withdraw from China as demanded or fight a war against the troublesome west. In 1937 the rapid rise of their allies Nazi Germany and Italy pushed them to opt for war.

'Well,' Professor Wang conceded, 'their assumption that taking over all China would give them unlimited resources and manpower, did not materialize. Instead it drained their manpower assets in Japan and forced them to go to a surprise attack on Pearl Harbor.'

It was no consolation for China in 1937.

Chiang Kai Shek in that hour in 1937 was the symbol of China as he stood there as the President and Commander in Chief of the Chinese Army. As a National hero he outfought the remains of the Warlord armies of Manchuria, Chahar, Jehol, Suiyuan, Tianjin and Hebei which surrounded the Chinese capital city of Beijing. Thus the Chinese capital of Beijing (Beiping) was in fact controlled by Warlords who were at the surface subservient to the Japanese Garrison Army which was called the Kwantung army.

I looked up at the face of David Pang. I had to help him but surely I can do both jobs together. The Boxer Treaty extended a lease of 99 years over Hong Kong to the British. But this lease caused the Hong Kong gangsters to move to America. A gang showdown is in the air with David a central figure in it. David Pang's society is old generation which in the old days engages in traditional gambling, smuggling and investment service for old migrants. But with the impending transfer of power in Hong Kong from Britain to China in 1997 a certain Hong Kong Guangdong gang is moving to California. A gang showdown is under way on ownership of property which belongs on paper to old original societies in China.

'Lily I have arranged for a one million reward if you find the figurines I employed you to find. Please conduct your search without distractions.'

'Miss one chapter and I have to go back again. No do not hurry me the figurines will be found I am sure.'

Professor Wang said, 'promise you will mark out the pages where there are important clues. I will help you to do the research.'

'Let us have dinner. There is a nice Café near the River gardens.'

We walked into the heavy traffic streets with hundreds of busy shoppers. The food is good and we had a good dinner.

I asked, 'Professor Wang, it was near here and Chapei that the 1- 28 1932 Incident was fought.'

'Yes, there was an American Naval Base just round the corner. All the factories were burnt out and the Chinese soldiers ran out of bullets. They were shot down anyway. Imagine?'

'Yes and then in 1937 suddenly the Japanese airplanes dropped leaflets from the sky. The leaflets say A one million men Japanese Army will soon land on Shanghai and then will march towards Nanjing. Chaos and everyone ran for shelter.'

David Pang interrupted, 'forget about ancient battles there is a current battle in Chinatown triads. A big showdown will happen in LA next month. It is a Triad showdown. Do your job Lily Shan.'

'Shut up and eat your dinner David Pang.'

'Have you finished your day dreaming? Will you help locate the lost treasure now?'

I smiled quietly and said, 'okay happy now?'

In the cool evening air, the Riverside Garden Café next to the Wusong River, was full of international tourists now that China is newly reopened for tourism. We three ate our food quietly as the soft music from a sound track played a haunting romantic song. But in my thinking I try to imagine how it was like this same River back on the eve of Japanese invasions in 1937. The old Shanghai was ruled by the Americans and British and the River was then called the muddy Soochow Creek.

Yes in 1937 the Shanghai population went about business as usual unaware that the Japanese war bombers are about to rain bombs on Shanghai. The Naval Warships are about to let fly artillery bombardments on the defensive positions of the Nationalist Army near Chapei. That was when and how sadly the now forgotten Second Sino Japanese War 1937 suddenly erupted in Shanghai. The public were never fully aware that the Japanese Army had caused the Marco Polo Bridge Incident at Wanping about 18 kilometers from Beijing (then called Beiping). Symbolically if the Chinese capital is captured China is conquered but the news media does not report it. It was remarkable that the public in Shanghai and Nanjing in 1937 failed to realize that a massive invasion is about to be launched by the Japanese Army and Navy.

But the pace of military action was unreported by the papers. The Marco Polo Bridge Incident was about a lost soldier who wandered into Chinese territory. Nothing as alarming as the capture of the Chinese capital was implied.

From the public view point it looked like an Incident not an Invasion till an explosion of artillery was fired onto the Chinese Army. Similarly in Shanghai a crazy soldier Oyama shoots airport travelers is not a war but rather a deception. The Japanese Army gives a list of unreasonable terms which they knew could not be complied with. Such as disarming the Chinese Army, no groups allowed in the city, and withdrawal from Shanghai. Meanwhile they arranged an armada of invaders on standby ready to into war.

David received a phone call which engaged him in conversations with the Shanghai branch of the society which we believe to be the Green Gang. He rejoined us.

'Well, my Shanghai cousin Pang says the name Gary Tang is known to his grandfather. It seems the old Pang from Nanjing was talking about a man named Tang who trained us in the Arts of War in gangland fighting. Attack is the best defense. Look that up Lily.

I dug up some old notes and found Gary Tang's signed notes.'

Attack by Stratagem/The Plan of Attack defines the source of strength as unity, not size, and discusses the five factors that are needed to succeed in any war. In order of importance, these critical factors are: Attack, Strategy, Alliances, Army, and Cities.

Tactical Dispositions/Positioning explains the importance of defending existing forts and towns.

Gary Tang's views were clearly written in handwriting in a discussion with Pang's grandfather in the Nanjing mansion of the old Green gang. I read it out to Wang and David Pang.

'Attack Attack Attack is the best defense.

My view of the Chinese Army and Japanese Army in this War of attrition is that the Japanese Army paid 90 % of their effort on attack when the foes faced each other in the first 3 months of the Campaign on the Shanghai Su Zhou fronts. The Chinese Army commanded by Chiang's Whampoa College trained Generals placed their reliance on Defense Defense even to the last man standing on the fortifications.

But from this point the Japanese changed their tactics faced with a Defense that stood up in Shanghai inflicting heavy Japanese casualties but the Chinese never changed or forgot to change or varied their stand to the last man until the last man fell. Many units including mine suffered 60-80 % casualty for a mindless reason.

By way of contrast the Left wing army (Communists) valued their fighting men, and preferred to run, ambush, run their units avoiding fixed position defense. They practiced fast mobility, disguised feints and rapid dispersal bringing it to a fine art.

It is unwise to plan a war based on 90% attack but the Japanese war plans did just that. Why? To overcome a massive barrier of 3000000 men defenders in Shanghai and Su Zhou there is no other way but Attack, Attack, Attack until the massive barrier is killed, burned and destroyed. Within a time period of three months which they had announced, they had to Attack at all costs.

Fortunately for them, this war is not a war of manpower but a war of war machines of destruction. Thus 1000 planes with 10000 bombs, 800 tanks and 500 artillery supported by Naval bombardment after four months of total war did break the backbone of the KMT defensive lines. Thus was the war lost to the Japanese Army.'

As I told the story to Professor Wang and David Pang they marveled at the hellhole that was Shanghai and Hang Zhou Bay as the Japanese desperately launched their two Invading Columns of a million men.

'Read on read on,' David Pang urged. 'These Japanese Invaders if they failed would have to commit hara-kiri as atonement for their failures.'

'Yes,' the notes of Gary Tang went on, 'but in Sun Tzu's Art of War, Attack and victory are two different matters. You can attack and not achieve victory.

A complete Attack which brings victory is where you swing the head of the enemy Army Commander in front of your men, This is the sweetest type of victory when his men see that you are their new king and surrenders in peaceful manner.

But with this Second Sino Japanese War, the Invading Japanese Army succeeded in capturing the Northern capital Beijing in 1937 and the southern capital Nanjing in 1938 and by the standards of Sun Tzu in ancient days that was as good as becoming the unchallenged new dynasty of this ancient kingdom.

The truth of this matter is that try and try again after more than twenty Big Battles they failed to capture Commander Chiang who unhappy but safe escaped to a new mountain capital in Chungking Sichuan. Wuhan was captured, Changsha was conquered and Guangdong was occupied, but Chungking was too remote to be captured. Thus Chiang the fallen Commander lives to fight another day. If he had kept to his original bad advice to fight in Nanjing to the last man, the Japanese would have achieved a big victory. If he had been captured or if he had been induced to accept a package befitting his surrender, China the nation would have fallen. But Chiang stubbornly fought on knowing the country was behind him. As an older generation fighter of Warlords he had hated their compromise with the Japanese.

One other principle from Sun Tzu's Book of War is to take care that the danger from the enemy's allies may change the fortunes of war.

Here the greatest mistake of the Japanese War generals was their alliance with Nazi Germany and fascist Mussolini. Their only similarity was the faith in military as a means to an end. The fear of Russia under Stalin, pushed them towards Nazi Germany with its strong show of Army and rearmament in defiance of the west. Otherwise they could not even communicate in their languages.

The Americans had always been exasperation in the programs of rearmament by Japan. When the 2nd World War began in 1939 and Pearl Harbor was attacked in 1941, at the same time as the American occupied Philippines war was declared.

As a formidable ally of Chiang in Chungking China the Japanese Army was hit with three or four War fronts. This sapped the energy of the Japanese Army and Navy and led to a slow but steady decline in war fortunes. Japan's fierce attack transformed into a costly defense and loss of their 6 aircraft carriers. With a world embargo on oil slowly but surely the fast mobility and attack capacity of a young Warlike Army turned into a rickety ancient infantry army. With desperation the Japanese Army now realized that Sun Tzu's principle to beware of strong allies of your foe is very true.

Therefore I can say on the eve of the Atomic bombs on Hiroshima that Japan's early victory in the Second Sino Japanese Wars provoked the Americans as ally of Chiang to send massive war aid to China and made the Japanese holding of China territory a massive drain on Japanese War resources. Japan had to feed and maintain a 3 million men army in China alone and as the civilian government had been kept in the background the military planners faced much trouble finding the finance to maintain a 5 million men army and at the same time having to replace their lost aircraft carriers.

Therefore I tell you my fellow secret society of Sun Tzu followers that the application of War strategy was practiced almost to perfection by the Japanese war time Army but despite their careful calculations they were defeated by Bad Feng Shui. Who can predict that the fortunate Chiang would have an American ally ready to spend billions of dollars to re arm his Chinese Army and fight the Japanese in mass infantry warfare on the islands of Guadalcanal, Saipan, Iwojima and Okinawa losing hundreds of thousands of American casualties?

Who else but the Americans?

Signed by Gary Tang.'

Before David and I left Shanghai for Hong Kong I happened to find a bit of interesting news. Who was this man a captain Chan in Kunming who worked as a soldier but was suspected to be a top drug smuggler who became a powerful secret society pole holder in Guangdong.

David was excited. 'He must be the uncle of Tiger Chan the man who is claiming to be the owner of the American smugglers farm.'

I said, 'maybe let us follow his trail back to Guang Zhou and see After post World War 2,there were two secret societies in Guang Zhou. The Sun Yee Oon was an old opium trading firm in the early 19th century which branched out into the control of opium houses. But I understand the new gang was a well connected Army officer who worked with an Army big shot.'

David said, 'Tiger Chan was his nephew I believe.'

'No matter what if they claim descent they must produce proof.' Your American ancestors were the ones who bought the American fishery warehouse with funds from the Green Gangs.'

chapter

THREE

Sino Japanese War in Beijing Tianjin

Gary Tang's Adventure in Tianjin
I alighted from the train at Tianjin station after a long journey on the Shanghai Tianjin Express train. In the morning mist a man came up to me.
'Mr. Gary Tang?'
'Yes I am.'
'Welcome to our city. I am Louis Fang your guide. I am staff officer for Commander Sung. Come get into my car, your hotel room is ready.'
'Tianjin is very warm, calm and leisurely paced city. I like this fresh country air.'
The hotel is in the foreign concessions zone of Tianjin with fine stone buildings and men dressed in western suits. In the distant there are faint sounds of cannons and airplanes can be seen flying from Japanese Aircraft Carriers towards the distant hills. A war is in progress in Lang Fang a town near Tianjin. Tianjin is truly a westernized city.

As I finished bathing I dressed up there was a knock on the door. The door opened and a skinny man in western suit walked in.

'What is this? Walter Kwok? I have not seen you since our University days at Harvard.'

Walter whispered, 'Gary I know you are on a vital mission but I am here to warn you about Louis Fang.'

He then told me to watch this Fang closely as he is a paid Japanese informer. Fang looked like an efficient officer well liked, But under the cover he is a trained spy working for the Japanese Kempeitai. His cover is known so I took a special effort to talk to him normally. Walter is working for ex Warlord Bao a master counter spy and special adviser to General Chiang. I made it clear I was a supporter not a major actor in this play of wars.

At the lobby I met with Louis Fang and a military figure named General Bao a former Warlord from Kwangsi south of Su Zhou. He is now a close adviser to code name General Kar Sher. We left the hotel by the back door and Fang drove us many miles to a forested temple outside Lang Fang. It is wartime. The Incident at Marco Polo Bridge is close to Langfang. The Japanese KTA informed the garrison one of their soldiers got lost at Wanping near the Bridge 18 km east of Beijing conveniently on the main North South Railroad Rail tracks. They then ordered the 29th Army of China to retreat out to a remote area and when the ultimatum was not obeyed they mounted a massive attack which gave them control of the North South railway to Shanghai. It was far from a mere Incident but a significant War Move as control of the Railway Transportation denied the 29th Army from any remote chance of reinforcement from the south.

The small army is in retreat from the Japanese advancing on the city on two fronts. The first Japanese Army attacks from Beijing's North west and the second attacks from Tianjin plains on Beijing's south east. After fighting for a week new Japanese troops arrived at the port to reinforce the Japanese attackers. The old forts at Tanggu have in history been easy targets for invaders. We drove towards the ancient temple which stands on a cliff overlooking the plains. The troops are brave, but bravery cannot win battles against well equipped armies. This war was lost on the planning tables of the Imperial Japanese army based at the Kwantung army base.

'Sir, a telephone call from the Beijing commander,' saluted Major Jiang. Fang nodded and passed the phone to General Bao.

'Sung come and meet at the old temple.'

The voice on the other side is that of Sung brilliant Commander of the Beijing and Chahar Army.

After an hour's wait a jeep rolled in. Sung entered the room introduced by Fang who poured a rich tea cup of tea for everyone on the oval table.

Bao said, 'our Chief wish to thank you for the brave defense of Beijing and Tianjin but he has bad news. Reinforcements are difficult and we must discuss alternative plans.'

'I need reinforcements and artillery support. They have thrown in planes and tanks to the attack.'

Bao stood up and calmly sipped his tea.

'What we learned from military school is now tested in the bloody battles. The Japanese 20th army is only 20000 men against our army of 46000 men. Further up the North West borders of Beijing we have an army of 60000 men under Generals Tang and Fu engaged in the Chahar war. This General Tang failed to defend Chahar against the Inner Mongolia Prince Te who was supported by the Japanese. He was a top general good at losing battles with the Japanese. It was only after the wars when he fled secretly to Japan to cure a serious illness that his enemies claim he was a collaborator. He died a painful death in a Japanese hospital. After their victory the Inner Mongolia puppet state was set up. The central Plains were or soon will be controlled by the Japanese by end of 1937.'

Bao's favorite subject came up next.

'But in the book of war strategy by Sun Tzu there are two strategies which our army has failed to match the Japanese. The use of fire what does it mean?'

He answered the question.

'Chapter 12 in the Art of War deals with fiery attacks taking the foe by surprise. Well the attack by fire is delivered through air planes, bombers, naval guns (at Tianjin ports) and truck mounted artillery pinpointing the location of enemy Generals with the aid of spies. We as for we our soldiers have to march on their feet from one zone to another. Their weapon is the small caliber rifles which is too old.'

General Sung shouted, 'precisely. Two of my best Generals counter attacked with foot infantry on the Great Wall battle lines. The Japanese lost thousands of foot soldiers but then, they hid behind the rocks and fifty thousand shells rocked the tent quarters of these two Generals who died from fragments of shells. If the battle was even and we had artillery and trucks in the mountains we could have over run the attacking army.'

I added my opinion to General Bao's.

'Sun Tzu the Master Strategist on War advocates the use of spies, collecting accurate information and deployment of secret agents but it is the Japanese army which practice this military art against us to perfection. That's how they pinpoint your positions.'

Bao continued, 'the Warlord armies in Chahar, and Rehe were terrorized between two evils, join us to defend our country as brotherly armies or ignore our call for reinforcements and be rewarded with honors by the Japanese army.'

General Sung coughed loudly. 'My apologies what is your point General Bao, Sir?'

'Well our army is brave but comprised of mere infantry against their tanks, planes and ships. Logically we should avoid direct army to army warfare until our brave infantry get planes, bombers and tanks in a more level fighting field.'

'I agree. When I see our men looking up the grey sky trying to avoid the deadly bombs from above, I feel so helpless. What can we do but watch as our comrades get direct bombs and their bodies sprawl across the muddy ground. Our soldiers had to march by foot carrying supplies but the Japanese Army got transported up the mountains then their artillery trucks mounted with guns shoot down on us from half a mile. Our poor rifles are helpless at half a mile. Then they send in their tanks and shoot up our front lines. Why don't our central headquarters buy tanks and planes and artillery so we can fight on equal terms?'

General Bao got lost for words. There are rumors that there is high level corruption in the Republican Army and millions are diverted into the foreign accounts of Generals. Big Generals have their own private armies. Some blame is paid on poor planning the ratio of armor to men should be higher. We should know where they plan to strike and what air support they have and tanks deployed. This became a critical factor when our defense holds up they apply precision air bombing and tanks to overcome resistance. The world economic depression of the early 1930's reduced military spending.

I stepped in to reply.

'General Kar spent his youth serving our leader Sun Yat San. In his young days he attended a Japanese military school. He used to raid the Kiang An Arsenal for ammunition. His role in defeating a dozen Warlords in the critical days 1913 to 1928 has earned him the highest respect. It may be a shortcoming not to spend big money on modern weapons of war and there is no excuse. We have to pay with many defeats to come.'

Bao added weakly, 'that is why we cannot send you reinforcements. They may be annihilated having to march by foot through the enemy controlled areas in Henan and Hebei.'

A gasp broke out around the table. To suggest defeat and retreat to the south is plainly implied by Bao whose nickname was the expert on War Strategy.

'But we are heroes of the people and heroes do not run from the Japanese army,' said Louis Fang.

'Yes yes,' Sung shouted, 'only cowards run.'

'There are two sides to the coin. If you knowingly pit your infantry in an unequal battle against the bombs and shells of a better equipped army you are sending your men to their death. It's true even though the reason is to defend the national Capital. History taught us this lesson when in 1898 the western powers with a column of 12000 men supported by horse drawn cannons, was able to defeat a Boxer Army of 50000. Our army is still relying on infantry in a modern war.'

Bao is suave in words and had us listening to his words of despair. It implies that the Japanese war machinery is too formidable.

'Talking about retreat in the height of a hot battle, my name is Gary Tang, from Shanghai and I carry a personal letter to you General from General Kar Sher, here the seal is unbroken.'

Sung opened the letter.

'Your request for reinforcements and artillery we are unable to meet. Bao will explain the reasons in war language.'

Bao said, 'reluctantly I must recommend that you arrange to retreat your army south to Henan or Hebei. If I send you an infantry army of 20000 there is danger that it will be attacked and decimated near Shandong where the Japanese have garrisons. The railway line is controlled by them Furthermore our intelligence information indicates there will be a massive invasion on Shanghai from the sea. No, General retreat does not mean that you will not take part in defending Nanjing. If they stage a surprise attack, on our beloved capital we need brave Generals like you. Your bravery shows that we may need you to command an army at Nanjing.'

Sung nodded and coughed heavily.

'My health may not last me long. This cough is getting worse and my doctors tell me there is no cure.'

I saw my friend Walter Kwok pointing towards Louis Fang. Suddenly I grabbed Fang by the neck and shouted, 'what have you put in the General's tea?'

'Nothing mercy it is not me.'

Walter Kwok walked up to Fang and ordered 'here drink this strong tea if you dare? And these are the chocolates and chewing gum you get for the General at the Harbin Depot. I want you to eat them all.'

Fang took the glass of tea but as he drank he accidentally let slip the glass. A second glass was made but this time he complained, 'if it is poison why force me to drink? I did not buy the tea as it was in the kitchen.'

'You were seen at Harbin collecting these things from the Depot 731. You picked up chocolates, tea, candy and black umbrellas. It is suspicious.'

Bao ordered doctors to attend to Sung.

'Arrest this man and put him on court martial trial,' he ordered.

I felt sad very sad as Sung was one of the most brilliant General. If we lose his service it is like the loss of 10000 men. The atmosphere became tense. We decided to keep this incident secret. General Sung's cough got better after he was given some antidote but every now and then he would cough badly. It was some sort of incurable poison.

The 29th Army fought bravely and retreated south towards Shanghai. But as they reached the Yellow River, the Japanese stooge Warlord Han Fu Qu refused permission to cross the Yellow River.

As for me I followed the retreat of the 29th Army. From 46000 men it had lost the bravest fighters. When we marched towards Hebei we were attacked several times. At last only 8000 remained. Sung ordered us to break up into 4 guerrilla bands and we trekked towards the Grand Canal. Sung's sickness went bad and after 10 months he died in Sichuan. I flew to see him in his ward.

He said, 'Many Generals have bravely died before me and many will follow. When I was a young boy that tyrant Yuan Shih Kai crowned himself the Emperor of China in March 1916. It was due to the great efforts of the southern Warlord Cai E that he was forced to give up his crown. You know after that General Cai E fell sick and there was no cure. He died a brave man looking like a skeleton. Goodbye.'

'General Sung if it is any consolation many good men have died in such mysterious situations. I remember Marshall Wu Pei Fuh also died mysteriously after drinking a kind of strong herbal tea.'

He nodded and smiled. He shook my hands then slowly I walked out of the ward. Sadness is in my heart.

We buried him with full honors and saluted a brave man who died for his country.

Tang's diary: the second Sino Japanese War 1937
Like a cat in the dark night
Roam the Ninja assassin
Slays the prey in the silent night
At dawn reverts to be a harmless man.

That is what I have to say about the Invasion of Shanghai which sprouted into the Sino Japanese War 1937. First a mad Japanese soldier ran amuck in the airport shooting people. When he was shot by airport security staff the Japanese Army called it an Incident and demand the Chinese Army to move out of Shanghai. When the request was refused the Japanese Army attacked the Nationalist Army near the Wusong River. Earlier in July 1937 the Beijing Tianjin War had broken out and the Mayor of Tianjin had been left without a soldier. He was allowed to slip quietly back to Shanghai where he Zhang Zhi Zhong now commanded part of the Shanghai Army. Zhang was a good General who likes to give press conferences on the eve of a war and perhaps that's why the Japanese allowed him to escape back to Shanghai. He obeys orders and is loyal to the Chief but his fault was he should have known it is fatal to send in a million troops armed with carbine rifles to defend against an enemy force armed with modern artillery, air bombers, tanks and naval warship bombardments. Can hand rifles shoot down planes, tanks and artillery barrage?

I was shocked when I saw the might of the Japanese military machine deployed at Shanghai's Soo Chow Creek and Huangpu River. The Yangzi River was deep enough for middle sized Japanese warships to navigate and bombards Riverside towns. The Japanese Army deployed 300 tanks, 130 ships and 3000 airplanes against the Chinese army's 16 tanks and 50 airplanes all destroyed.

As a comparison of the two armies deployed, the Nationalist Army had 3300000 troops in 75 divisions and 9 Brigades, 250 airplanes and 16 tanks.

The Japanese Invasion Force had 300000 troops in 8 Divisions and 6 Brigades, 3000 airplanes, 300 tanks and 130 naval ships. A second task force of 400000 waited in several stations including Japanese ships, Taiwan, Qingdao and Korea to land at Bay of Hang Zhou. It may have been a million men army as the Chinese had 1.5 million men defending posts dotted around the Shanghai Su Zhou twin cities. Their propaganda leaflets dropped from the air warned that a million men army invasion force will attack Shanghai. The master plan involved Divisions from the Beiping War and Shanxi War after these Divisions had conquered Shanxi they advance south west towards Wuhan.

Their soldiers were indoctrinated with cultural and martial superiority over the inferior Chinese. This indoctrination caused a mad rage when the inferior soldiers or unarmed civilian should kill a Japanese soldier. Japanese soldiers are aware of the military tradition which was called 'the three kills'. Kill all, Burn all, and destroy all. It would be an unbearable shame to suffer defeat at the hands of the Chinese. Some of them would commit Harakiri if they stare defeat in the face.

I heard rumors about senseless kill kill, applied to civilians, rape and mutilation applied to women, girls and old women, and burn burn mass burning of Chinese captured soldiers after they were shot. Another wild rumor circulated by mouth was that there were two Japanese soldiers competing for the title of who will chop off a hundred heads of Chinese soldiers or civilians. It was confirmed when I read some Japanese newspaper reports with pictures of these soldiers swinging their swords.

What caused this mass madness and thirst for revenge against the Chinese villagers? One possible reason was the wild circulation by Japanese military about the slaughter of 10000 Japanese soldiers. In an early stage of the Shanghai Invasion, a disaster befell when the Nagoya Division tried to land in the night near Chongming one of the big islands on the Yangzi River. By error they landed on a well protected River shore and the Chinese soldiers machined gunned a majority of the soldiers. The rotting bodies of thousands of dead Japanese soldiers lay in no man's land as fighting was very heavy in the first two months. To the horror of the Japanese soldiers as they saw on No Man's Land, their brother soldiers' bodies rotting, they spread and circulate this horrible act of killing of Japanese soldiers. Soldiers get slapped by their superiors for small mistakes. It is a crime of insubordination or indiscipline. Soldiers are superiors of Warlord soldiers including the Nationalist soldier, thus when the soldiers see Nationalist soldiers shooting down Japanese soldiers their reaction is to slap or execute the inferiors. Revengeful is their heart and respect for the Nagoya Division soldiers whose bodies lay on the disputed landing zone.

The anger ignited the soldiers. Further their military had bragged in Japanese newspapers that in three months by October Nanjing will be captured. But as at November the Shanghai defenders were fighting hard whilst their ammunition lasted. Then on the eve of the second Invasion force's landing at Hang Zhou Bay commanded by a former governor and commander of Taiwan, Yanagawa, wild rumors circulated among the soldiers that the Invasion of Nanjing may be called off by the civilian government in Tokyo.

The military spread the rumors about rotting soldiers. It angered the common soldiers and renewed efforts were made to complete the conquest of Nanjing and avenge the rotting bodies of soldiers. Slowly there were whispers among the invaders Kill all, Burn all, Destroy all. The word stress and trauma is not known in the indoctrination of Japanese Infantry but the word Shame, Revenge or Hara-kiri is well indoctrinated in them. A soldier's duty is to die by fighting and survival is seen as cowardice. It is believed that some ultra Nationalist patriotic officers of Japan might have spread the rumors. One of these officers accused of or believed to be inciting troop hatred was a man named General I Cho who was known to have founded an ultra Nationalist Society. He committed ritual suicide in later world war defense of Okinawa.

There were no explanations for the brutal killing of civilians, raping and mass killing, burning of dead and property burning except that it was an ancient war punishment called the three All strategy induced by a big crime. Widespread Insubordination, indiscipline and killing of Japanese soldiers by inferior Chinese soldiers is certainly a punishable crime. Even a Japanese soldier who commits indiscipline or insubordination would have been punished severely by his superior. Slapping and tongue lashing is common. Down the chain, the Japanese soldier is the superior of Warlord soldiers including Nationalist soldiers. (A second occasion when the Japanese Army in China ordered the vengeance of Kill All Burn All and Destroy All was when the Chinese Leftist Army launched the Hundred Regiments Ambushes in Central China.)

The second column for beach landings at Hang Zhou Nay was headed by Yanagawa of the 10th Japanese army. This column in October was ordered to march inland quickly towards Nanjing flanking the Defenders in the Su Zhou line. All along the scorched earth invasion path of destruction, the Japanese Soldiers committed savage killing of civilians, rape and mutilation of women and girls in the villages, burning of property and robbing of valuables and instant killing of captured soldiers, decapitation and mass grave burial.

When the Japanese troops arrived at the outskirts of Nanjing in early December General Tang En Zhi realized that his order to hold to the last man is unrealistic and survival to fight another day is possible. Troops were simply abandoning their posts, had no chance of winning. Chiang maintained that General Tang should continue to stage the defense.

On 7 Dec, the Japanese Army announced internally that soldiers who commit "illegal acts" and "dishonor the Japanese Army" during the conquest of Nanjing would be severely punished. Whether this was obeyed is doubtful. On 9 Dec, the Japanese Army arrived at the Nanjing's city wall, and demanded surrender within the following 24 hours. No Chinese envoy appeared, and at 1300 hours, the two commanders concluded that the Chinese were not interested in negotiating, and gave the order for attack.

The Japanese 36th Infantry Regiment attacked the heavily-defended Guanghua Gate at 1400 hours, which was manned by some of the few experienced troops at Nanjing. During the course of the afternoon, the Chinese troops at Guanghua Gate increased to 1,000. Concrete pill boxes, tankettes, and the usage of fire inflicted large numbers of casualties among the Japanese, but greater firepower eventually overwhelmed the Chinese. By nightfall, Japanese mountain guns had destroyed part of the gate, and the Japanese troops poured in and drove out the last of the defenders.

Tang gathered his divisional commanders at his headquarters, and the group unanimously decided that winning was impossible. Tang refused to be the sole blame for losing the battle, thus he had everyone sign the document from Chiang noting that retreat was only permitted when absolutely necessary.

On 12 Dec, Tang decided to go via Yijiang Gate in the north the only gate still in Chinese control; he left the city. It led to the retreat completely breaking down. Many men found their commanding officers disappearing, and began to flee in all directions in panic.

As organization broke down, so did discipline; American journalists Frank Tillman Durdin of the New York Times and Archibald Steele of the Chicago Daily News reported witnessing Chinese troops looting shops, while others threw away their uniforms and weapons in an attempt to disappear into the civilian population. The Chinese 36th Division at Yijiang Gate, still holding on to orders to block any retreat (Tang never revoke his previous order before he fled the city), confronted the units attempting to pass through the gate. Thousands of Chinese troops crowded inside the Yijiang Gate, and the 36th Division troops opened fire on those they considered deserters. Some began to push in even greater panic, and many were trampled to death. (See http://ww2db.com/battle_spec.php?battle_id=38)

By the end of December the Japanese Invaders arrived at the walled city of Nanjing from the South, South west, North East and along the Yangzi River. The Nationalist defenders had moved out of the city at night headed by General Tang En Zhi a former Warlord. There followed a wild month of chaos which in history is called the Nanjing Massacre. There occurred mass rapes and mutilation of women and girls, mass shooting of surrendered soldiers and senseless killing of unarmed civilians. The zone of Safety was broken into by Japanese soldiers. The city was administered by the military but later the Chinese run Restored Government of China was set up under the Chinese politician Wang Jing Wei who was the rival of Chiang Kai Shek. There are conflicting accounts and estimates of the number of victims killed in the Nanjing Massacre but the estimate of 200000 or 300000 was most often quoted.

Today there are Memorials, photos, books, War crime records, and Computer sites and museums in Nanjing city where the horrible pictures of the Nanjing Massacre can be seen.

From these sites the casualties were reported as 333500 including 250000 KIA and 91 planes lost. There were reports of higher casualties based on the assertions that 60% of the defenders perished. The Japanese casualties was 92640 including 70000 KIA 85 planes and 51 ships lost.

It was a bit irrational to order defending divisions to hold a fixed defensive position and fight to the last man when the enemy is known to use planes, mobile artillery, tanks and ships to support their troopers. The Japanese Army seemed to have knowledge of this irrational strategy after two months of intensive and costly attacks. The Confucian military culture and mentality emerged whereby thousands and thousands of soldiers are ordered to fight to the last man at the post when in fact the men were sitting in fixed positions armed with rifles while 1000 Japanese planes bombed them, 300 tanks fired and attacked, 300 naval ships send rockets from the deep navigable Yangzi and Huangpu River and trucked artillery rained thousands of shells on them. The Japanese Army moved in trucks but the Chinese soldiers moved by their own feet. Personally I believe the Japanese Army funds were used to buy arms by serious people bent on real war but some officers of Chinese military were believed to have bucks on the side with westerner and local firms as a form of pay off.

It was heart breaking for me to hear the bombs rain on our poor troopers and divisions of brave soldiers and these officers die from the technology of the Japanese war machines. I made out a table by the River's Cliffside and prayed for their brave lost souls. But no Commanders dared to criticize their top decision maker who would view any dissent as Confucian insubordination. Such was the Confucian centric military culture of those times. Bao the paper military strategist and his boss Li did try to suggest that the Defensive lines be moved inland but it was not heeded. The only explanation I can think of is that codename Kar as Commander was pinning his hopes on western intervention or even the civilian government in Tokyo. That did not come sadly for half a million brave defenders and when their rifle ran out of ammunition after three months of fighting they faced certain death. The retreat order came and they simply ran helter smelter towards Nanjing where 20000 defenders waited with poor prospect to stop the Marauder Invaders.

I have to report sadly it was a big Chinese defeat the biggest defeat in history of two famous cities Shanghai then Nanjing. The commander's blind order to stand and defend to the last man caused very massive loss of manpower among all fighting divisions. Shortage of ammunition can be expected but it was fatal after three months of intense fighting. When it happened it induced a type of fear that it was hopeless fighting planes and tanks and truck mounted artillery wave after wave. It was unjust for the Confucian Patrician to demand such an impossible fight.

There was massive retreat and surrenders after three months of fighting without rest. The Defense of Nanjing became desperate as 10000 officers (40%) had perished and most divisions had lost 60% manpower. On 8 November a general order to retreat was issued at last. But Nanjing fell after two weeks of fighting. The Central China Army of Japan took control of China.

After the chaotic Nanjing Massacres over a three month period it was later proclaimed that the Restored Government of China under Wang Jing Wei was restored. The word 'restored government,' suggest that the Japanese Military thinkers viewed the war as a breach of the style of government made famous by Viceroy Yuan Shih Kai almost one of master and servant but hidden from the view of the civilian home government.

What was the aftermath of the second Sino Japanese War of 1937?

On a personal level I experienced something called sadness, emptiness, sympathy, mortal pity and goodwill towards the victims of the Nanjing massacre.

I attended a meeting in defeated Nanjing where I met a western pastor the Reverend John Magee, a member of the American Episcopal Church Mission. He described the massacre in these words which was presented to a court at the War Crimes trial later and published.

'On December 13, about 30 soldiers came to a Chinese house at #5 Hsing Lu Koo in the southeastern part of Nanking, and demanded entrance. The door was open by the landlord, a Mohammedan named Ha. They killed him immediately with a revolver and also Mrs. Ha, who knelt before them after Ha's death, begging them not to kill anyone else. Mrs. Ha asked them why they killed her husband and they shot her. Mrs. Hsia was dragged out from under a table in the guest hall where she had tried to hide with her 1 year old baby. After being stripped and raped by one or more men, she was bayoneted in the chest, and then had a bottle thrust into her vagina. The baby was killed with a bayonet. Some soldiers then went to the next room, where Mrs. Hsia's parents, aged 76 and 74, and her two daughters aged 16 and 14. They were about to rape the girls when the grandmother tried to protect them. The soldiers killed her with a revolver. The grandfather grasped the body of his wife and was killed. The two girls were then stripped, the elder being raped by 2–3 men, and the younger by 3. The older girl was stabbed afterwards and a cane was rammed in her vagina. The younger girl was bayoneted also but was spared the horrible treatment that had been meted out to her sister and mother. The soldiers then bayoneted another sister of about 7–8, who was also in the room. The last murders in the house were of Ha's two children, aged 4 and 2 respectively. The older was bayoneted and the younger split down through the head with a sword.'

Much later in official trials after the World war (reported in Wikipedia) another case was reported. According to Navy veteran Sho Mitani, 'The Army used a trumpet sound that meant "Kill all Chinese who run away" Thousands were led away and mass-executed in an excavation known as the "Ten-Thousand-Corpse Ditch", a trench measuring about 300m long and 5m wide. Since records were not kept, estimates regarding the number of victims buried in the ditch range from 4,000 to 20,000. However, most scholars and historians consider the number to be more than 12,000 victims.'

There were 600 other cases which were filed later at the War Crimes trial. It is a war which cannot be forgotten.

Sadness I felt
For the victims of war,
But the Chinese people
Endured their sufferings
Went on living hurting
With stress in later lives

The historians came in with their detached observations. It was a case of the ancient military culture which happened in Japan. But times had changed. The fight for independence had caught the imagination of the colonized peoples, even from within the Colonial countries such as Britain and America. As for China it was the abandonment of the Confucian Landlord Gentry symbolized by the Warlords and the demand for democracy symbolized by Sun Yat San and the Nationalist Party, Kuo Min Tang. Slowly the Confucian teaching in schools to revere the old family heads and king Emperor was discontinued. In its place college education took roots and the theme was for democratic rule by a government which will address the needs for justice and fair play for people.

On a national level I was unhappy at the great defeat and Japanese Military takeover of Chinese cities. Many people were critical of Chiang that as a leader he allowed the first blooming flowers of Chinese patriotism to die fighting against tanks, warplanes, artillery and warships armed with simple rifles in hand. This to me was Confucian Military Blunder of the highest order. Later on in the Civil War there were key desertions and surrenders of top Commanders because of his poor war strategy which use up soldiers as cannon fodder. But it was a romantic old slogan fight to the last man.

At the same time I was happy and forgave him when I heard that there were Face to Face Battles at Wuhan, Changsha and Suzhou where his military fought with modern tanks and gave back what they had endured for decades. In all there were 22 Battles not including the Burma front campaign where the Chinese Army assisted the Allies. Somehow he regained peoples' confidence. Hope was held by millions that the Japanese Army somehow will be defeated.

I stayed in Chungking serving as Intelligence Logistics officer. It was like a different country with its green hills and truly an army city. I planned to return to Shanghai as soon as things settled down. Everything and everyone was waiting for some thing to happen after the lull in Chungking.

My feelings were mixed. Chungking is safe from Japanese air strikes and land armies. Where are our Armies though? No not in Chungking but hidden away near the big provincial cities such as Changsha, Su Zhou, Wuhan, Nanchang. Their supplies come from Chungking though.

Chapter

FOUR

Armies transformed by war

What happened to the ancient style and deep tradition of these two Asian armies? They transformed themselves into modern armies. In 1937 they entered the Second Sino Japanese War as proud Armies seeking quick regional victories. But eight years later by 1945 both these Ancient Type of armies emerged out of the war thoroughly transformed. The answer lies in the rapid changes in technology and government control of the military machines. Technology has outdated the ancient war goals. Army technology pitted the Zeros against the armada aircraft carriers which moved stealthily against the Japanese oceans. The Air Force rushed through a new Super Bomber which could fly 2000 miles and back without the need to stop at fueling stations in the Pacific oceans. As for the Japanese Army as they lost fine ships and planes the holdings of a million square miles of land proved an impossible burden rather than a valuable asset. The scale of World War 2 requires budgets beyond what the ancient small army can afford. The secret development of a powerful atomic bomb was lost when Germany surrendered but then it was redirected against Japan when it became clear they will die rather than surrender.

Was there Third Sino Japanese War? If so when did it begin?

If America did ally with Chiang's Army as the supplier of arms, tanks and training to a great extent then it is not a confined Sino Japanese War. If Chiang was left to his own devices, then capitulation would be a wise choice rather than face an Army with the massive War Machine. Sometime in 1939 the minor aid given to Chiang's army in Nanjing grew significantly when the Chinese Army deployed hundreds of tanks, bombers and artillery in the Battles of Wuhan, Nanchang, Su Zhou, Changsha and the central plains. That in my view would be a changed war with a new ally.

It was in early 1939 that I met an old friend in the Chungking hospital. He looked like a skeleton but clearly it is Captain Chung now promoted to a Colonel. This brave guy saved our lives when he led the Japanese pursuers away from our hiding place.

'Where have you been?' I asked.

'I took part in three major battles but as usual we lost tens of thousands of men. Lost the battle and fled. In 1938 the Japanese advanced on Wuhan city from two Pincer directions. The first Pincer was from the north at Hebei and the second pincer came from the east at Nanjing which had just been conquered. They sent in tanks and captured Wuhan circle of outer rings. The centre was captured without a fight. But again Chiang escaped the dragnet. He retreated to the western city of Chungking in Sichuan.'

He looked at me.

'Loyalty is a quality which can change from white to red. Chiang has held the two camps Technically trained military Generals like Chen Cheng, Tang En Bo together with the ex Warlord Generals united. At least they fight back.

'I shall be loyal to our army and our country. The Japanese hopes Chiang can buckle under the pressure but so far he has fought back.'

He looked at me with a half smile, 'Our Commander Major Wu he has changed sides and now sits in Prison in Wartime Chungking. Can you believe that? He has joined the Leftist Army.'

I felt confused because to me he is the Army. Yet the widespread corruption inside our Army was exploited by the Leftist Army. Major Wu regularly complains about corruption. When his friends were executed for planning a coup in wartime Chungking, he was jailed for one year. After his release nobody knows where he is.

I must confess the Leftist Army won many hearts by criticizing Chiang's failure to drive the Japanese Army out of China. Their message to deserters like Major Wu was, 'We pledge our Generals shall fight for China and even die for our country. Yet the right wing army fights for themselves and gather money and lands for their own cliques and clans. Their army is robbed by corrupt practices of rival Generals. They do not fight for China but for themselves.'

To little people like me, we will never be rich and have no chance to be corrupt so we simply follow orders.

The Japanese Army had conquered the Burmese hinterlands but their greatest goal to capture Chungking eludes them. Several attacks against Chungking in Sichuan were repulsed at Changsha east of Chungking and northwards Wuhan. However it was not possible to attack Chungking from Wuhan mainly because of the great winding Yangzi River steeply descending from the highlands. The soft mountain gorges are difficult and impossible for an invasion army.

The next battle was at Nanchang the approach to Wuhan. They were stopped at Xiushui River then waited for reinforcements, and started the second invasion with 120,000 troops. After an artillery barrage Japanese troops began crossing the Xiushui River.'

'I heard you people released the waters of the dam and caused 500000 drowned.'

'Yes.'

Somewhat embarrassed, he continued 'the third battle was at Changsha in Hunan in 1939. We drove them off after a hard fight and counter attacked. They reached the outskirts of Changsha but was then encircled and lost a hundred thousand men. I hear there will be a new attack on Changsha next year because it is so vital in supplying smuggled goods to Chungking in Sichuan.'

'Good thing Colonel Chung, if Chungking falls, we are finished.'

'Yes I agree Colonel Gary Tang. I fear the China I grew up in Shanghai is no more. The Japanese troops occupy our cities and the puppet government of Wang Jing Wei act as a veil of secrecy. Even the International Zone of Shanghai governed by the Americans and British are feeling insecure with thousands leaving while they can in great numbers.'

'Chung, do you know that the Americans will come in to this war on the side of Chiang? There is a Marine Base at Soochow Creek. I fear 500 Marines is not sufficient. They will be interned as prisoners should war breaks out.'

Chung replied in guarded tones, 'No official comments but I can see American Agents busy in Shanghai collecting information. How can they help China, all the coastal cities are firmly in Japanese hands? There are no tanks or planes or new gun produced in China to replenish the Chinese Army. Instead I hear rumors that the great iron and steel works in Manchuria are being used to build five aircraft carriers and a thousand planes. What are they to be used for if not to open a new War somewhere in some new zone? They dream of repeating the Russo Japanese War where they were victorious over a western country.'

'That is the problem. China's resources and war machines have halted production so where do Chiang get his planes, and tanks and artillery from if not the Americans.'

'I agree with you. But the ports on the coast of China are closed surely there is no way smugglers can smuggle such large items into these Chinese interiors.'

Chung whispered in my ears, 'well Gary there is a rumor that the Americans are supplying war machines to Chungking via Yunnan.'

'Yunnan? There is no factory for guns or trucks in Yunnan! You are mistaken.'

He grabbed my hand. 'Think carefully since you are an expert on War Strategy. The Army must be supplied or else the Kuo Min Tang or Chiang's government will fall.' He continued with an exciting tone, 'Opium has been smuggled to the Shanghai Opium Dens from the hills of Yunnan since the 1920's. It is easy to use the opium trail.'

True the opium trail from Yunnan to Shanghai has been well known. But the sheer logistics is unbelievable. It would take a ship to unload in Rangoon and truck the guns and tank parts to Mandalay 800 miles. From Mandalay there are only tracks going up the high mountains to the border of Yunnan. If the British are allies of America and China it can be done but the cost is unimaginable. Still it is possible if the Chinese Army has patriotic soldiers, or manpower they can hack a zig zagging road up the mountains to the border town of Lazio. From Lazio it is an easy trip into Yunnan the trail of drug smugglers for many decades.

But then what would the Japanese Army do? Would they pursue the American financed arms smugglers from the ports of Burma and thus cut off the Army of Chiang from Burma? Yes they would but the British control Burma. Would they go to war with Britain?

It depends on their budget and their war chest surely.

Colonel Chung read my mind and said, 'the Nazi Germany has signed a pact with Japan as Ally. Germany has signed in 1939 a non aggression treaty with Russia which protects Japan in the Far East. It is possible the Japanese Army will invade Burma because they are trying to win over Chiang as an ally. Yes if Chiang comes under the Greater Asia Co Prosperity Sphere, it will be a great victory for a great Army. As for the Americans they will support Chiang fully to preserve the hope of the Chinese Republic.'

'You are in Intelligence Chung I am merely in Logistics. So I will rely on your judgment.'

For the next two weeks I visited my friends in American Logistics as well as our headquarters sections. Slowly I ascertained that indeed they have allocated a budget of 5 million US dollars to build a Highway in the sharp winding hills from Lazio in Burma to Yunnan in China. Word has spread that the Americans have allocated 100 million Lend Lease Aid program to help China to rebuild its Army and Air Force. I believed with good reason that somehow the Japanese Army will invade Burma in the near future because it has vast resources at its disposal.

The Japanese strategy in Sino Japanese Wars

A Japanese General of high rank was Assistant to the young Commander of the Kwangtung Army. The confidential leak from a foreign news service was circulated among Chinese Army Generals. I managed to get a copy of it.

The Japanese Colonel was observed complaining at a secret conference of Generals in the Japanese Army in China.

'I do not understand, boss, when the Shanghai and Nanjing wars ended in November 1937 our victory was as clear as the sun shines, we had captured the two Chinese Capitals Beijing and Nanjing. China is in our hands.'

'Yes,' his boss was raging in anger. 'The best factories ammunition and plane factories and tank builders found in Shanghai, Manchuria, Guangdong and Nanjing is now in our hands. Why then does General Chiang still have tanks and planes which he sends against us in the Battles of Wuhan, Nanchang and Changsha?'

The Boss raised his voice, 'We captured Guangdong in October 1938. With that victory we had the whole coastal cities under our control. Militarism is the means Control of this ancient land is our end. These western countries are playing us as fools. We must act against them. Our attack against key cities such as Changsha and Wuhan was successful but the Chinese Divisions retreat just out of range. They then regroup for another battle.'

Another famous Japanese General experienced in battles stood up, 'Our Army Planners reports that we have three big problems.

First to annihilate the Chinese Republican or KMT armies we must stop them from getting planes and tanks supplied from Burma into Yunnan. This means we invade Burma if necessary. To annihilate the Chinese Republican or KMT armies is our top priority.

Second the Americans have placed a world embargo of oil on Japan. Our planes and ships may stop in the ocean. Further all war supplies are embargoed. It is an invitation to war no less. The solution is to invade the countries in South East Asia and Burma where oil is plenty.

Third the Americans have given notice of an ultimatum for us to Quit China and Quit the French Indochina which the Germans gave to us in 1939 when they were victorious over the

French. Regrettably it is unavoidable they will go to war with us and attack our Navy. Strike first Strike deadly and Strike to Win that is the code of honor in a war. Fortunately our ally, Nazi Germany has started invading France and England. The British are weakly defended in Asia. In Malaya they have an army of 8000 men, we can fight them. In Singapore they say the fortress is invincible. I shall see to it that Singapore is taken.'

The Second Sino Japanese War of 1937 and that of 1939/40 is different because China is now supported by western countries. It is best described as a 3rd Sino Japanese War we can say. The biggest difference is that the Chinese Generals were taught to stop deploying into pitch battle against the Japanese infantry divisions moving on feet without air, tank and artillery support. Never again will they send troops without mobility and ordered to fight to the last man as in ancient comic books. Why did this happen?

Chiang's national army is supported by the old Warlords who provided Warlord Armies as allies. It is not fully integrated nor commanded by a strong central command. The mark of these old Warlords is that they were trained on methods of war from ancient times almost always infantry unsupported by a modern Air force defense nor tanks and artillery. Many of them bravely sent themselves to destruction.

Chinese viewpoint

With his back to the wall Chiang rallied support from former rivals and they fought as one. There were Face to Face Battles at Wuhan, Changsha and Suzhou where his military fought with modern tanks and gave back what they had endured for decades. In all there were 22 Battles not including the Burma front campaign where the Chinese Army assisted the Allies.

The conquest of Burma by the Japanese Army in 1942

Burma is rich with oil fields. But the true reason they invaded Burma was connected with the massive military aid sent to Yunnan from Burma. The Burma conquest by Japan was aimed at the supply of war weapons including tanks which were reassembled in Sichuan. In December 8th 1941 the Japanese Army Navy launched simultaneous attacks on Pearl Harbor, Manila Bay in the Philippines, Malaya, and Singapore. In January 1942 they launched attacks on Burma. In Burma they attacked Rangoon then advanced on Mandalay in the foothills. With a force of 100000 they fought and defeated the British Army and Chinese Divisions nominally under Stilwell. At Toungoo a Chinese force of 90000 men supported the British Army but the Japanese targeted them with 50000 casualties whilst the British Indian division suffered 14000 casualties.

The Japanese Army had achieved their major aim deny the use of the ports of Rangoon to supply the Chinese Army via the Yunnan route. With the Burma Road closed the Americans turned to the use of airplanes supplied from India being flown by air to Yunnan. Chiang had to be kept supplied to keep them in the war. The answer was to fly supplies from British airfields in Assam, India to airfields in Yunnan, China. The flight path was a hump that means flying towards the Himalayas then turning towards Yunnan. These flights came to be known as the Hump flights. Planning for both the Hump flights and, the construction of a new road from Ledo, to Yunnan kept the Chinese Army supplied. On July 4, 1942, the Flying Tigers (Aviation Volunteer Group) were renamed the China Air Task Force (CATF), a component of the 10th Air Force, and were commanded by promoted Brigadier General Chennault. He had served as a volunteer commandant of the Flying Tigers for many years giving air support. One of his most famous battles was in the Burma wars when the dreaded Red Dragon Armored Battalions had trapped the Chinese Warlord of Yunnan's troops in the Battle of the Salween River. Six Chennault P-405 planes came to the rescue and bombed the Red Dragon tanks to destruction in the wild Burmese jungles as reported in the American Time magazine.

Final Invasion of Chungking 1942

In War the point of final victory is the final act, you have to finish of the enemy. By a brilliant stroke the Japanese Army in China had invaded Burma and stopped the supply of war materials through Burma and Yunnan. They began to plan an invasion from Hunan's west towards Sichuan to capture the capital Chungking.

The invasion of Sichuan starts from northern Shanxi central Hubei and southern Hunan. Heavy aerial support and bombing of Chongqing supported the advance of Japanese Army with

500 tanks and 500 planes and bombers with 120000 soldiers. It coincides with the siege of Leningrad by Nazi Germany.

According to reports for the Americans General Chiang Wei-kuo has warned that should the invasion by the Japanese be successful, the Japanese planned three steps. First extend the puppet government in Nanjing throughout China. Second persuade Chiang to join the Co Prosperity Concept. Third appoint a Japanese Governor General similar to Korea. Count Ito the former Prime Minister of Japan was the first Governor General of Korea when Korea was known as the colony of Chosen. He was assassinated by a crazed Korean in 1910. Four individuals who held the position of the Governor-General of Korea were former Prime Ministers of Japan due to its importance.

Hence the Japanese Army in China had not abandoned the old ambitions of empire. Their ambitions were fanned by the expansion of a new idea Totalitarian discipline which breeds no tolerance for dissent. The mighty Nazi Army rearmaments program followed by victories in Europe impressed them. Their own rapid victories in Singapore, Malaya, Netherlands East Indies, Philippines and Burma had boosted their morale. The reunification of China is a dream coming true.

'A Governor General?' I asked. 'Would China go the same way?'

The American Liaison Officer looked alarmed. Slowly he replied, 'No because the fight back by China was fairly intensive and two major operations the invasion of Sichuan 1942 and the invasion of central Plains in the Ichi Go Expedition in 1944 were counter attacked with heavy casualties by the Japanese Armies. Our country has sent an Adviser Stillwell, to give material assistance.'

The Americans felt that a counter invasion not commanded by Americans would fail. This was based on the Japanese invasion of Burma when cooperation broke down. The Chinese Army felt that their own national Army should not be commanded by Americans.

This General Stilwell's relations with Chiang specially was difficult as he felt there was widespread corruption By this time the Lend Lease Aid program to China was close to 1.5 billion and Americans questioned the waste. In the Burma war Chiang had promised a 95000 army but the British and Stilwell treated the offer cautiously. Further when the Japanese attacked and out-flanked them the British Armies retreated towards Imphal inside India leaving the Chinese army stranded on their own. The Chinese felt the White man mentality was too much to stomach. The British trusted their own Indian Brigades Asians who kowtow to the Sahib. The Japanese tried to take advantage by accepting an alliance with Chandra Bhose an Indian National who wished to drive the British out of India. The Japanese Asian Co Prosperity Sphere appealed to Asians who hated colonialism such as Wang Jing Wei of China.

America is strong Ally.

The best of allies was Chiang and America in the war years. There was a touch of vinegar though in the relationship between Chiang and the American Adviser Vinegar Joe Stilwell. In the Time Magazine of 13-12-1944 some reporter asked 'why was he recalled? The answer was not forthright from FDR.

. 'It's a simple fact. General Stilwell has done extremely well. I'm very fond of him personally.... You all have your likes and dis-likes because you're all extremely human. Generalissimo Chiang Kai-shek and General Stilwell had had certain fallings out, oh, quite a while ago; and finally the other day, the Generalissimo asked that somebody be sent to replace General Stilwell. And we did it.... It's just one of them things....'

Here there was a strange conflict Chiang was seen as holding back his army for a final fight with the Left Army but the Americans mind set were too influenced by immediate need to win over the Japanese. They somehow forgot the Communists were their ultimate enemy. This funny state of affairs went on and Chiang was left alone to fight the civil war. It was not until their ally Chiang was forced to retreat across the Straits of Taiwan that they renewed the old policy to be Taiwan's protector.

Stilwell himself was absorbed with the idea that with the Chinese soldier and American Arms they can overcome the im-age of weak Chinese soldiery. For example, in the Time Maga-zine article it was said.

' In China, Stilwell developed one deep conviction that was also a deep compliment to the Chinese nation: he believed that the straw-sandaled, underfed Chinese soldier, properly equipped, trained and led, was the fighting equal of any other nation's soldier. He was sure that he could create a striking force with Chinese manpower and U.S. weapons that would drive the Japanese from China. After Pearl Harbor, he got the beginning of a slim chance to test this belief.'

It was a dream that can never be. At the last minute the KMT realized that the Leftist Army would get US supplies and fight under him (Stilwell) too. This more than anything resulted in the recall of Stilwell who appears to be unable to reconcile with the China Christian values in the KMT Army. China owes Stilwell a debt for he was pioneer of the Aid to China idea.

Therefore looking back on events Chungking was a time when the two sides of a civil war bide their time for a bigger War.

By 1944 the confidence of the Japanese Army in China was shaken.

One of the last battles saw the Japanese Army fighting for control of China's roads and rails from Manchuria to the central plains down central China to the Vietnam border.

The Battle of Changsha (1944), (also known as the Battle of Hengyang or Campaign of Changsha-Hengyang) was fought.

This rail corridor would control the smuggling of arms to Chungking the Wartime capital. In June 1944 the Japanese deployed 360,000 troops (and air or sea support) to invade Changsha for the fourth time. In public no one was aware that there was one hidden strategy that is American bombers stationed behind the Chungking airbases are being used to bomb the Japanese Home Islands. A quick thrust and attack could put them in danger.

The Chinese National Revolutionary Army's Tenth Corps under General Fang Xianjue repelled attack till 3000 survivors out of 17000 remained. For one time in the war, the Japanese casualty exceeded the Chinese. Chinese divisions tried to relieve the defenders at the city of Henyang but failed.

Unfortunately for the Japanese the high cost of men lost together with the loss in July 1944 of an island at Saipan resulted in the loss of prestige and the resignation of a top Commander H Tojo.

88

The Japanese eventually captured Tenth Corps commander Fang Xianjue, who surrendered Hengyang on 8 August 1944 after his Tenth Corps was decimated from seventeen thousands down to three thousands of wounded men. This concluded the Campaign of Changsha-Hengyang. General Fang was rescued by a daring raid and brought home to Chungking. General Fang was decorated personally by Chiang in a war short of heroes. He lost 14000 men defending Henyang in the Battle of Changsha but for the first time the Japanese casualties were higher.

After the Battle of Ichi Go in central China in 1944 which was a Chinese reverse Stilwell tried to place the Chinese army under his direction. Chiang responded by asking for a replacement advisor. It would appear that if there is an alternative plan to finish the Japan Army in China then it would be safer to do so and continue to use China as hunting bait to tie to up the Japanese Army of 3 million in China.

The negative public opinion in the U.S. that followed caused the U.S. to lose confidence in Chiang vs. Japan. Instead the U.S. redirected all its war plans to the Island-hopping offensive in the Pacific.

The Japanese successes in Operation ichi-Go had limited effect on the war. From the Chinese territory of Henan down south to the Vietnam border their army swooped on every city. It was not a war but a show of force in China just as their positions in the island hopping towards Australia is meeting some stiff real fighting back. U.S. could still bomb the Japanese homeland from Pacific bases. The Japanese control the cities but not countryside. The increased size thinned out the Japanese lines. Chinese Army forces were able to retreat out of the area, and later sneak back to attack Japanese garrisons.

Sichuan Invasion

The successors did no better when they tried to capture Chungking from three directions. Again they suffered big casualties out of a total force of 90000. In April 1945 Japanese divisions invade a heavily defended city in Zhejiang in the west of Hunan, to open a path to Sichuan. The Changsha Battle involved a nearby city Hengyang. The troops were intercepted in an ambush by the Chinese National Guard and were almost completely wiped out, and China regained some of its territory. By this point, the course of the war had turned to retreat?

This was a great failure for the Japanese Army. But it warned the Americans that Air Bombers based in Chungking are not highly safe if they planned to bomb Japan from China.

Japan's conquest of South East Asia

After the 1937 Nanjing war, the Japanese started building five new aircraft carriers and hundreds of destroyers, airplanes and bombers which were used a few years later to attack on the same day, Pearl Harbor, Singapore, Philippines, Burma and Netherlands East Indies later renamed Indonesia.

Would they stop at Netherlands East Indies later renamed Indonesia? No, quietly they sent battleships to the islands approaching Australia such as Papua, New Guinea, Solomon Islands, and Guadalcanal in Midway Islands all forming a ring of islands bordering Australia. Airfields and army posts were built on these islands, Why? For what, purpose? The Japanese Naval Power at that point in time around February 1941 was after bombing Pearl Harbor the biggest Naval power in the world. It was lurking around the Solomon Islands with six Aircraft Carriers hunting four remaining American Aircraft Carriers. The High Oceans was on the point of a huge deadly duel between the great Japanese Admiral Yamamoto and his Commander in chief Admiral Negumo. The Japanese Army was chasing a final showdown with the famous American General MacArthur who is commanding new US troops from the USA in Brisbane Australia after being forced to evacuate from the Philippines in December 1941. The Japanese Naval Fleet of six Aircraft carriers with double that number of support battleships and destroyers were hunting the American three or four American aircraft under the command of the little known Admiral Nimitz.

But by these times the Americans have enough experience of Mushashi's War strategies to find a warlike response. Their heads were reeling when they sat down to realize that the conquering Japanese Army's impressive record was they had conquered the greatest Asian nations such as Korea, China,

Vietnam, Singapore, Malaya, Philippines, Burma and Indonesia. Bravely they had attacked by surprise the strong American fleet in Hawaii The only force stopping them from landing on Australia are the remaining American Navy and the American and small Australian Army. It is likely that MacArthur then and there decided if they attack strongly then we counterattack strongly and stubbornly, if they fake and divert then we fake and divert as well. If they hop from island to island to encircle the Northern Australian cities, then we hop from island to island until we reach the Japanese Home islands. But first we must understand their War Strategy.

DECEPTION

When you cannot be deceived by men you will have realized the wisdom of strategy.—Miyamoto Musashi.

DISCIPLINE

When you have attained the way of strategy there will not be one thing that you cannot understand.—Miyamoto Musashi,

ATTACK

Once at the enemy, you should not aspire to just strike him, but to cling after the attack.—Miyamoto Musashi,

The moment the enemy relaxes attack strongly and quickly.—Miyamoto Musashi.

When the enemy makes a quick attack, you must attack strongly and calmly aim for his weak point as he draws near, and strongly defeat him.—Miyamoto Musashi.

Attack in an unsuspected manner, knowing his meter and modulation and the appropriate timing.—Miyamoto Musashi,

It was still a Sino Japanese War because from the vast iron and steel, coal and slave labor in China comes the hundreds of Japanese carriers, ships and airplanes. The support given them by the traitorous Chinese puppet government was incalculable. The Chinese Republican Army and to a lesser extent the Left wing Army kept the 3 million Japanese Army in China unable to be diverted for overseas wars. But the cost the cost was millions of lives lost. The Americans valued the alliance with Chiang's China though the corruption was exceptionally high and general knowledge but Chiang personally was not corrupt merely his supporters.

How to finish the Japanese Army in China?

The aims of the Allies were to finish the strong seemingly invulnerable Japanese Army of the world war.

Back in Manchuria the dark moon shone as the well guarded army headquarters slept with pride dark figures crept in and opened the safe. They were Ninjas Chinese Ninjas. Swiftly silently they disappeared into the darkness of the night. The next morning the night guards at the gate shouted at the figure dragging a smelly cart.

'Halt,' who goes there?

'Night soil,' the Night soil man said.

'Get out fast I can't stand the smell.'

Eventually the stolen plans ended up with American Advisers in Chungking and once again I managed to buy a copy on the restricted market.

The transcript of the Japanese Army meeting has bad news as well as good news.

The former Deputy is now the Commandant and the former Commandant is now a Minister.

'I congratulate our former Commander Tojo as he is now in Tokyo. War has been declared on us but we have sent six aircraft carriers plus 400 planes, torpedo bombers and air bombers to disarm the American Fleet in Pearl Harbor. Here are their losses.

Japanese Attack Fleet
6 aircraft carriers
2 battleships
2 heavy cruisers
1 light cruiser
9 destroyers
8 tankers
23 fleet submarines
5 midget submarines

American losses at Pearl Harbor
414 aircraft4 battleships sunk
3 battleships damaged
1 battleship grounded
2 destroyers sunk
1 other ship sunk

3 cruisers damaged
1 destroyer damaged
3 other ships damaged
188 aircraft destroyed
155 aircraft damaged
2,402 killed
1,247 wounded

The second good news is that we have achieved victories and conquests at Singapore (where the 2 British battleships Prince of Wales and Repulse have been sunk), Malaya, Philippines, Dutch East Indies and British Burma

The third good news is that preparation to surround and invade Australia is progressing well. We have set up Air Bases and Ship Bases at Rabual, Bougainville, Guadalcanal, Solomon Islands, Midway Island and Port Moresby. Armies will be deployed later for advancing into Australia.

The War Strategy of Island Hopping back to Tokyo

I was alert when I realized the Americans have proposed an alternative way of finishing off the Japanese Army. They would avoid the risks of staging air bombers in Chungking in view of the Ichi Go movement of Japanese armies. The trouble between General Stilwell and Chiang was a personal thing but it is now affecting their country's interest. Therefore to finish off Japan through the Chinese Republican Army advancing into Manchuria and Tokyo is risky.

Chungking was a troublesome hotspot because Chiang had to pursue two conflicting duties. Firstly he needed to arm the Chinese Army to fight the Japanese. The Americans pushed for this strongly. Second he needed to but secretly kept it from the Americans that a future battle against the Communist Army will have to be fought. In secretly pursuing this goal he was accused of corruption, suspected of diverting war supplies and his generals were accused of corruption.

The Americans especially Stilwell failed to understand that Chiang's KMT Army had a Christian Chinese dominance. The American missionaries for a hundred years had a special closeness to China. This developed into a pro Chinese KMT Nationalist support which called for Chiang to head the counter attacks.

The American report was influenced by simple war logic. If the KMT Army cannot give overall command to the Americans, then victory cannot be guaranteed by a counter attack. Their confidence in Chiang's army to do the job against the Japanese was very low. Slowly an alternative strategy commanded by Americans themselves began to be proposed to finish the Japanese Army.

To repulse the Japanese Army hop from island to island right up to the Japanese Home Islands. Then it happened their island hopping resulted in the capture of Saipan bringing the service of a base to service or refuel their air bombers. At the same time their industry was rushing through a super bomber that would not require any refueling.

Japanese naval defeat at the Battle of the Coral Sea

The Coral Sea is on the seas bordering Australia and its islands are vital to host an attacking Japanese army before the launching of invasions. In early 1942 the Japanese Navy headed by 6 aircraft carriers and the American fleet spearheaded by 3 Aircraft carriers played hide and search destroy games in the coral seas. If the Japanese Navy is destroyed the Japanese invasion is finished. Not only that the Japanese Army in the Asian countries will be strategically trapped and with only infantry they will be no match for the long suffering Chiang's Republican Army.

At the Coral Sea the Americans prepared to attack a Japanese held island airfield with planes from aircraft carriers. The cunning Irish streak in Americans knew that several Japanese aircraft carriers were waiting to finish off the remaining two American Aircrafts Carriers hiding in the Coral Seas.

With the advantage of having decoded the Japanese secret cipher code, it was a fishing bait hoping to split the formidable 6 Japanese task force of Carriers which remained fully intact for final destruction What were they hunting? The American Aircraft Carriers USS Enterprise and US Yorktown were their main targets. The Japanese sent in two Aircraft Carriers which had taken part in the Pearl Harbor attack. The American torpedo planes, from an Island attacked the carriers and the American carrier came in with airplanes and bombed the carriers causing serious damage. Two Carriers Shokoku and Wukoku were seriously damaged and reduced the Japanese superiority from 6 to 3 Carriers as the command carrier did not take part in sea battles.

Sun Tzu's disciple a man named Chu Ke Liang in the Period of Three Kingdoms described how the use of hundreds of War Boats by Cao Cao of the Wei Dynasty nearly destroyed the allies Kingdom of Wu and Shu. So in the Pacific Naval Battle between the Japan Naval Carriers and American Naval carriers whoever controls the Oceans through wiping out the opponents fleet, shall rule the oceans. They hunted and counter hunted each other in what is known as the Battle of the Midway Islands at edge of Australia near the Coral Sea.

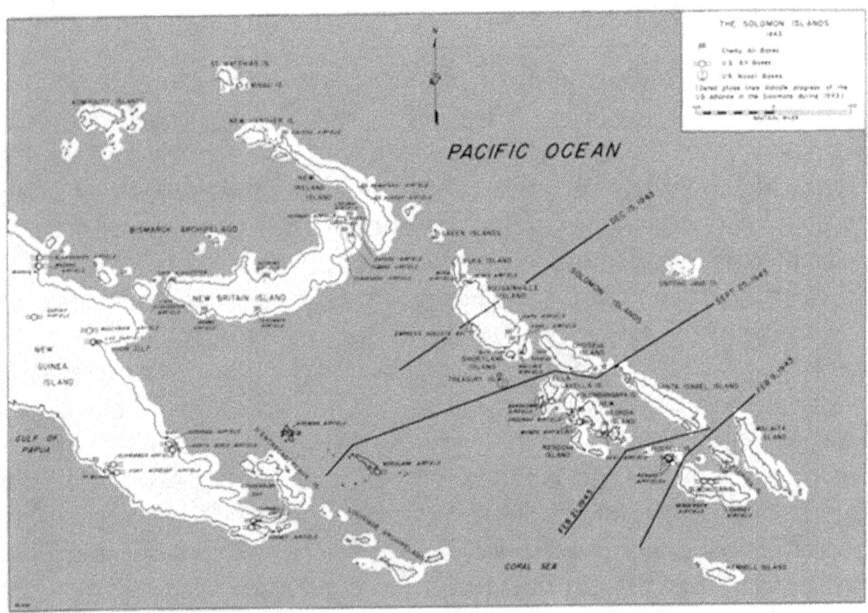

Figure 9: Coral Sea source: www.wikipedia

General MacArthur led the Land army of the Allies defending New Guinea but eager to invade the Japanese held Philippines. The Japanese are led by H Imamura based at Rabaul in Guinea. The Japanese 18h Army was responsible for Japanese operations on mainland New Guinea and Papua.

The Japanese plan of attack was based on a task force of naval ships. First Mobile Force (4 carriers, 2 battleships, 3 cruisers, and 12 destroyers) would raid Midway and destroy its air force. Second Fleet (1 light carrier, 2 battleships, 10 cruisers, 21 destroyers, and 11 transports) would land 5,000 troops to seize the Midway from the American Marines.

This planned seizure of Midway will draw the American carriers into a trap for the First Mobile Force would engage and destroy them. Afterward, First Fleet (1 light carrier, 7 battleships, 3 cruisers and 13 destroyers), would complete the destruction of the American Pacific Fleet.

From a Japanese viewpoint their fleet of four carriers, two light carriers, 11 battleships, 16 cruisers and 46 destroyers would fight the Americans with only three carriers, eight cruisers, and 15 destroyers. Victory is assured.

The old naval story is retold. After the three Japanese aircraft carriers with planes had bombed Midway Island badly they returned to their carriers. But as their bomber planes landed the aircraft carriers were vulnerable because the planes had to be moved to permanent park bays. The deck of the carriers was at the most vulnerable point. Hundreds of American torpedo planes and bomber squads attacked the Japanese Carriers but there was a fleet of Zero II's which mowed them down all of them. In desperation there was only a slim hope. High flying bombers with precision bombing were just out of reach of the Zero fighters.

The High flying dive bombers plunged down on the startled Japanese, who were turning into the wind to fly off their own striking warplanes. Flight decks were crowded with armed fueled planes, and hangar decks held other planes and much unstowed ordnance lie on deck. A bomb will ignite a series of explosions on the carriers. Multiple bomb hits ignited fatal flames on three of the four Japanese carriers, which were immediately put out of action. Japanese victory in this battle of the Midway Islands was gone with the half destroyed aircraft carriers. As they burned, consumed by explosions, Kaga and Soryu sank late in the afternoon. The Akagi followed them before dawn the next day. Thus it happened that at the Battle of Midway Island in 1942 the preparations for the Invasion of Australia was dealt a fatal blow when five of the six Aircraft Carriers which destroyed the great American fleet at Pearl Harbor seven months earlier had been destroyed. Two of the Carriers Shokoku and Wukoku had been disabled at the Battle of the Coral Sea a month earlier. If these two were in Midway the battle may have changed.

Entrapment

Who trapped who? In fact the Americans had broken the telegraph code of the Japanese. The Japanese Naval fleet felt ashamed that two carriers were seriously damaged and set towards the Midway Island to destroy that base. They were ignorant where the American Carriers were ignorant that the Carriers were setting a trap waiting out of sight near Midway Islands while the Islands torpedo bombers attacked the Carriers of the Japanese First Fleet which mobilized air bombers and annihilated the islands home base.

As the Japanese airplanes landed on their home carriers the American bombers and torpedo caught the Japanese carriers by surprise. They prepared and fuelled their airplane bombers to strike back at the Americans. The waves of Torpedo bombers were destroyed by Japanese Zero fighters. But a squadron of high flying bombers dive bombers sent their bombs onto the four Japanese Aircraft Carriers. The Akagi, Soryu, Hiryu and Kaga were destroyed and sunk.

Admiral Yamamoto ambushed

Another setback was the shooting down of Admiral Yamamoto who is a brilliant war strategist. Without the secret code breaking it is felt by many that they would have been victorious. On the morning of 18 April, despite urgings by local commanders to cancel the trip for fear of ambush, Yamamoto's two Mitsubishi G4M fast transport aircraft left Rabaul as scheduled for the 315 mi (507 km) trip. Sixteen Lightning's intercepted the flight over Bougainville and a dogfight ensued between them and the six escorting AGM Zeroes First Lieutenant Rex Barber engaged the first of the two Japanese transports which turned out to be Yamamoto's plane. He targeted the aircraft with gunfire until it began to spew smoke from its left engine. Barber turned away to attack the other transport as Yamamoto's plane crashed into the jungle.

The crash site and body of Yamamoto were found the next day in the jungle north of the then-coastal site of the former Australian patrol post of Buin by a Japanese search and rescue party, led by army engineer, Lieutenant Hamasuna. According to Hamasuna, Yamamoto had been thrown clear of the plane's wreckage, his white-gloved hand grasping the hilt of his katana, still upright in his seat under a tree. Hamasuna said Yamamoto was instantly recognizable, head dipped down as if deep in thought. A post mortem of the body disclosed that Yamamoto had received two gunshot wounds, one to the back of his left shoulder and another to his left lower jaw that exited above his right eye. (http://en.wikipedia.org/wiki/Isoroku_Yamamoto)

With sinking heart the Japanese High Command felt that the one man who could give them a fair chance against the American Navy was gone. These Generals knew that the victory of the Russo Japanese Wars 1904 was owed to the Navy. Now their brave Navy is gone. Their Army fights alone.

The Island Hopping war

The Island Hopping war started In mid-November, 1942 the U.S. Navy fought the Japanese at the Battle of Guadalcanal, when the Japanese attempted a major reinforcement of troops. In this four-day battle, the U.S. Navy foiled the reinforcement effort, and only 4,000 of 10,000 Japanese troops reached land. The Americans had war experience against the Nazis in the European World War 2. They counter attacked the Japanese with well laid plans.

Island hopping war began when the Japanese sought to conquer Papua and New Guinea. A chain of island stations centered on New Guinea was built. But they encountered fierce resistance from Australian Army forces. The Japanese drove the main forces out of towns where they waged a guerrilla type jungle war. The American Marines tend to invade Island after Island.

Figure 10: Guadalcanal, Solomon Islands.
(http://www.guadalcanal.com/images/troops_
blackandwhite_147k.jpg)

Island Hopping War/ Battle of Bay of Leyte
The return of MacArthur to the Philippines took place in 1943 after the Battle of Leyte in the Philippines.

The War Strategy had now been reversed as the Japanese Army without or deprived of Naval Support is fighting a war as Infantry against the war machines of the Americans. The relative poorer Naval Strength of the Japanese was later estimated as follows:

Battle of Leyte Philippines
American Naval strength
8 fleet carriers
8 light carriers
18 escort carriers
12 battleships
24 cruisers
141 destroyers and destroyer escorts
PT boats, submarines
About 1,500 planes
183,000

12,513 killed
38,916 wounded,
33,096 non-combats

Japanese Naval strength
1 fleet carrier
3 light carriers
9 battleships
14 heavy cruisers
6 light cruisers
35+ destroyers
300+ planes (including land-based aircraft\)
117,000
About 95,000+ killed
7,400–10,755 captured

If Naval strength is the prime criteria then Japanese naval defeat was assured from the start. They had built many ships after breaking the naval parity treaty to enable them selves to build more carriers. These new ships have been destroyed or lost and their navy is now badly outnumbered. The Americans now possessed an overwhelming superiority in arms and numbers; this, coupled with the lack of Japanese opportunity to retreat or reinforcement, means no plausible scenario in which the U.S. could have lost the battle.[

The last Islands where bitter war was fought were at Okinawa and then Iwo Jima. As the Japanese show that the rate of casualty of the invaders will be high was there an alternative.

The secret Manhattan project was about ready for deployment. A War strategy of mass destruction has arrived. Would this weapon of mass destruction be used?

Enola Gay is a Boeing B-29 Super fortress Bomber newly deployed for very long distance flight with little refueling.. On August 6, 1945, during the final stages of World War II, it became the first aircraft to drop an atomic bomb on Hiroshima Japan, and caused extensive destruction. The Japanese Army surrendered to the Americans. The bombing of Hiroshima and Nagasaki may have saved many lives on both sides by causing the surrender of

Japan before an invasion of the Japanese main island was carried out. Estimates were as high as 7,000,000 Japanese civilian and military casualties and 500,000 American military casualties.

To the horror of the besieged Japanese Army one bomb wiped out maybe 200000 citizens at Hiroshima. A second bomb wiped out Nagasaki where the weapons of ships were reduced to dust. The skins of victims were burned and scarred beyond medical treatment. Someone had to stop it all. Someone did and the Commander in chief did. That was how Japan announced surrender.

Was the two Asian Armies transformed by the wars?

The Japanese Army recognized that the Intervention of the western powers was inevitable. Way back in history in the Russo Japanese War three countries forced Japan to give up the seizure of Port Arthur. In 1932 the west intervened to outlaw the seizing of Manchuria and declaration of Manchukuo. In 1945 the end of World War 2 forced them to abandon their conquests in China and Korea and South East Asia. It was a bitter transformation perhaps for the better when they were encouraged to engage in trade not war.

In the case of China hopefully the strategy of defending to the last man standing was transformed. The strategy of combined naval, air and land war fronts improved just a little bit but to what extent it is doubtful. Later in the civil war battles, the divisions did not perform well.

In the case of the Japanese Army, the ancient values such as the spirit of Bushido were always retained though it was adapted and changed by the use of war technology. The greatest transformation of the Japanese Army was their understanding of how the Chinese Warlord cliques worked. They sensed the instinct for personal self survival held by Warlords. The respect accorded to them in turn made them happy to treat the Warlord as good subordinates. This partly explains the practice of staging Incidents. In most cases the threats posed by an Incident was enough to get the other watching Warlords to toe the line. But by the start of the 1937 War new Warlords such as Young Marshall Zhang Xue Liang were more concerned with the country than the State.

However towards the end of the World War, the Chinese Armies proved to be more, crafty avoiding a fixed defensive position which it defends to the last man.

The Japanese Army was ever watching and ready to forgive a small Warlord clique should they breakaway silently imperceptibly from the grand alliance. Chiang's advisers, was watching too but in the case of the Yunnan Warlord they pounced too quickly. Warlord Long Yun's personal sway over his loyal Yunnan Army later led them in the civil war to join the Communist Army. In the case of the Sinkiang Warlord they were correct and prevented a major defection by the far western based Warlord bordering Mongolia.

Such maneuver was unknown to the western allies who believed Chiang had a unitary command. Chiang grasped by instinct the human machinations behind Sun Tzu's War strategy better than anyone. Warlords tend to prefer self sufficiency and pay lip service to control from the centre. Even Sun Tzu would find it a problem of war where war machines are of key importance more than infantry strategy. Yet the KMT Army tends to lack emphasis on planes, tanks, mobile artillery and mobile speed. Air power was very weak.

Thus technology, war technology was important but ignored and neglected.

These weaknesses were critical because the KMT Army had an important mission to defeat the Leftist Army. Yet they relied mainly on infantry. Even when they had air support the communication was weak and basic.

The control of the China Railway is paramount to Japanese War Policy. In the Russo Japanese War their control of the South Manchurian Railway strengthened their military grip on the Province. They ensured that the trunk railway between Beijing and Shanghai and Beijing and Wuhan is in their hands.

Later, in the Civil War the Left Wing or PLA made sure they controlled the railways to deny besieged forces the chance of reinforcement. This was critical later in the Liao Shen battles between the KMT and PLA armies in the north in Manchuria. In the Song mountains and Huai River campaigns if the tough KMT Generals Huang and Qiu had reinforcements they would have been saved.

chapter

FIVE

Chungking ally against ally

For 7 long years Chungking in Sichuan became a war time capital of the Chiang government. It was the Japanese Army's military successes that drove Chiang to seek sanctuary in the Wild West provinces. For centuries these far west provinces were ruled by Warlords. When the wartime capital moved far west to Chungking Chiang had to accommodate the Warlords into his Army. Chiang was skilful at building alliances with these secret society types of power holders but the Americans especially a major General who was his adviser was not fully acquainted with these Secret Societies, their oaths, bonds and rules. Relentlessly the Japanese Army destroyed Army after Army hoping that Chiang would reach a breaking point. But to its surprise every time a soldier fell two would jump in for a national cause.

Some critics said Chiang could only hold the balance, amongst the major cliques and factions but not organize them into a single force. Who were these cliques and factions? Nobody knows because after all every General paid lip service to the slogan, 'Chiang is our Chief Commander, we are loyal to the President, China and our countrymen.'

Chiang himself came from the school of hard knocks. In the years before 1911 he was Sun Yat San's soldier section head, having graduated from a military college in Japan. He was mixed up with the Green gang and hunted by the Warlords of Nanjing. There was a famous incident when the Green Gang joined him in suppressing a Gigantic Master Strike by the Left Wing in Shanghai it was called the Shanghai Massacre. Truly it was a class war between the Confucian Gentry and the Peasants. The gangsters are uneducated but they are an integral of the Confucian Gentry culture and big holders of much land. Many other Warlords ruled their own Provinces having loose ties with the central government the most notorious being Yang Zhi Shan, Zhang Xue Liang and also Li Zong Ren, Long Yun, Sheng of Sinkiang and others. Chiang's inner circle is his former cadets at Whampoa military college where he was Principal. They are now major Generals but many are accused of corruption. They were spied on by the Japanese spies as well as the Communist Spy network. Chiang's greatest contribution was his ability to balance these forces into a single Army to fight the Japanese.

When I straggled into War time Chungking with Wu and Chung we registered our army credentials. I was sent to work in Logistics Intelligence; Major Wu was promoted and assigned to Propaganda. Captain Chung was sent to Army Intelligence.

Slowly I settled down and learned that Chungking and its western neighbor city Kunming were centers of smuggling gold, drugs, human trafficking and thriving Casino towns. Life in war time Chungking is dull but the war is always in our minds.

One afternoon a man knocked on my office door.

'David Kung I was told you are in America?'

David told me he was on holiday and Maggie had told him I was seeing Grace Lu.

'Anything wrong? I think she is beautiful smart and a good talker.'

David informed me that 'Chungking is a city of spies, gamblers, smugglers, opium gangs and high level corruption.'

'I can tell you that but you have to be in the front line to know how it is like.'

I took out an envelope from my desk. 'Here David, have a look unsolicited bribe money being left on my desk. The Green gang rules supreme in these highlands. Their local front man has a regular dispatch of goods which I have to store in the green store. The paper work has to be signed by our stores. What is in these boxes I shudder to guess?'

He then told me 'that with secret societies in this city they are very powerful with important members sworn as blood brothers in the military, casinos, drug smugglers and bankers all part of a sworn brotherhood. With the front line there are rivals who hijack a gang's consignments and shoot to kill if necessary.'

He wrote a name on a piece of paper. 'Check this man out. He is very interested in Miss Grace Lu and whatever Mr. Yunnan Tung wants he gets.'

There is no need to investigate for in my Logistics work I knew that Boss Yunnan Tung is a powerful man in Yunnan. He is rumored to be in drugs. As I finished work, I got ready to close the workshop. Suddenly a dozen local gangsters pushed me down on a chair. Their leader said, 'my boss has a girl friend who works in a gold shop in town. He wants you to stay clear you understand?'

I said, 'Who are you? Does your boss love the girl or is he a love mad gangster? As her good friend I want to make sure she is not forced into anything.'

'My name is Yunnan Ma and you are Colonel Tang?'

They roughed me up but then a tall middle aged man came in. He looks tough a man who commands attention. His steely eyes looked at me.

'My name is Boss Yunnan Tung owner of Casinos in Shanghai, Hong Kong, and even America. I want you to know that I am really interested in Grace. She has spoken of you kindly. Will you give up trying to win her heart? You get in her way you know.'

'Let me tell you I am her friend and wants to be sure you do not love her and leave her like you have done to a dozen girls. If you treat her unkindly I am here to be her friend.'

'Look here Colonel Tang I do not now how but I love Grace very much. David is her good friend and David's mother Lisa is my good friend. If money is what she needs there is no problem.

But I want you to not disturb her. I have been helping her sick mother in Nanjing she needs an urgent operation.'

I explained to him that 'I am just a good friend but I must see that she is not abused. As you know your past reputation in Chungking is notorious. I hope you can reform for her sake.'

Though we are good friends I have been calling on her too often. It gets into her way sometimes.

He said, 'Yunnan Ma the Dicer tells me you have been digging into information about my past life. I have killed people for lesser offence. Will you stop your nonsense?'

I nodded.

'Good any friend of Grace is a friend of mine. If you need help see Yunnan Dice okay?' He wiped his gloves, 'Goodbye then friends?'

'Yes yes,' I mumbled.

After he left his deputy kicked me.

'Whatever Boss Yunnan Tung wants he gets. You are a thief of hearts. My name is Yunnan Ma. They call me Dice it Ma.'

He slapped another hard slap on my cheeks.

'Don't upset my big boss. What he wants he gets.'

I kept on seeing Grace though as I can see she was confused and flattered by the attentions of a powerful man in the west where the networks are extensive. She was lonely and needed a friend and good advice.

She told me, 'he came with his girlfriend the actress Butterfly Ying to buy a diamond ring. Somehow they quarreled. He began to see me for dinner and gave me expensive gifts. Love? He is not capable of loving anyone.'

She took me to the caves near the river. 'Do you know why David left me for another girl? It hurts so much but the rich gentry are like that, we poor peasants are their playthings, Gary.'

'David had been warned off by this powerful businessman, warlord's friend and fabulously rich big boss. Their word is law in this wild west.'

'But it is not fair. Like an emperor he boasts of a dozen concubines, but me, I cannot stand this power crazy man.'

I took her hands in mine, 'Grace you are a rare ancient beauty with the grace of sweet smelling perfumes. If you need any help or someone to talk to I shall be always at your service.'

Grace took my hands and her eyes were burning with angry frustration, 'If he wants me I shall let him but mark my words I shall be like the great Empress Wu of ancient China, and instead of being ruled by him I shall rule him like a great Queen. Yes that is the answer. Will you help me Gary?'

I was impressed. 'That is the spirit the best way to control your feelings is through his pocket. David and I are watching over you. He is good at money collaterals. I suggest you hatch a plan to change all the gold in his pockets to land and property in a safe haven such as Hong Kong.'

She gave me a peck. 'I shall try that.'

Front line? Those words were used by David to describe Grace's work. At the front line Grace deals with clients in Shanghai and Nanjing taking orders for wholesale goods like precious stones, diamonds and gold. Smuggled clothing from America and Europe pass through the underground network. Security guards are a tough job which Grace controls with the assistance of her contacts with Yunnan Kung. But the smuggling of currency is the most profitable and risky. I help with the logistics aspect where we have surplus transport services.

I kept an eye on this Big Gang Boss of hers. He ruled over Night clubs Casinos and underneath the cover he is reputed to be a drug and diamond smuggler from Burma to the cities of China. When the Japanese Army invaded Burma he set up a foreign diamond and gold chain of shops in California.

I rode my cycle to the Officers club. The Bar was perched overlooking the River Jialing with its winding river course giving a splendid sight of Chungking. The confluence of two rivers Jialing and Yangzi was a beautiful scenic attraction for me. My usual drinking friend Major Chan a skinny fellow from Guang Chou near Hong Kong was talking with a northerner.

'Come let me introduce you General Kwok here is from Guang Chou or Canton.'

'Walter Kwok what a small world? Where are you serving nowadays?'

Chan rebuked me, 'He is a General, General Kwok of the American Volunteer Group of Air Fighters.'

'Remarkable I heard you were in the Air Fighter Bomber Squad that attacked the Japanese Red Dragon Armored Corp in the Salween River battle in Burma? How is the American Air Marshall Chennault helping our War effort?'

Walter Kwok is a self made soldier. He came from a family of teachers won a scholarship to the prestigious Harvard but his fortunes fell when his sponsor the Warlord Feng Yu Xiang was chased from the Warlord post of Shandong. Warlord Feng ought to know better than to sidetrack from his post as Japanese Army sponsored Warlord of Shandong. He remained a controversial leader neither a Confucian nor Communist but a leftover from Yuan Shih Kai. His famous year was when he escorted Pu Yi the Qing Emperor from the forbidden Palace to the Tianjin Imperial Mansions. He aligned with Warlord Yan Shi Shan to fight the National Revolutionary Army in the Central Plains War 1930 but was played out by the crafty fox. To be a true patriot it doesn't pay. Earlier in 1926 for a brief few months he allied with Sun Yat San and the Fengtian Warlord Chang Tso Lin. The Japanese Army acted against his ally when Chang Tso Lin's train was bombed by sabotage. Feng Yu Xiang drifted along the two opposing streams of Chinese Nationalist Army against the Chinese Communist Army. He controlled the big army called Guominjun, but then in 1930 he began to rebel against the KMT Army when they sought to take over his army. The central Plains war lined up his army and his allies Yan Shi Shan and the southern Warlords Li Zong Ren, Bai Chong Xi and Tang Zheng Zi. Chiang's Army was manned by his Whampoa graduate Generals. Warlord Feng Yu Xiang lost and his army was absorbed but his allies Yan, Li , and Bai made pacts with Chiang and survived. The Warlords were defeated though they emerged in new clothes as allies of Chiang with the armies intact. This war costs billions and got the new Government of Chiang into financial difficulties.

Warlord Feng died on a Russian ship near Odessa, still seeking to make deals, a sad end for a former Christian Warlord.

Walter Kwok's loyalty to Feng is intense and he is under suspicion to be plotting a coup against Chiang's Whampoa Generals inside wartime Chungking.

He asked me, 'You can join us for a better China.'

There was an inner anger in him when I replied, 'Feng is a good Warlord but still a Warlord. My lot is to do my duty not re write the rules. I will fight the Japanese Occupation Army and

Chiang may not be perfect but he is our only hope. I cry when I remember General Sung poisoned by a slow death.'

The Communists build up a potential coup unnoticed. But the intellectual lobby has now become a growing worry in war time Chungking as outlet for expression is limited. One of the accomplishments of the Communist sympathetic intellectuals is the holy oath to the country. While the KMT Army Generals grow rich and corruption is leveled at them the Communist's Army made appeals for the country to 'fight for the country against Japan without enrichment.' Thus even though Chiang and the KMT are the successors of Sun Yat San who is seen as the living oath to the country, the Leftist fifth columnists claim to be the true fighters for the country. It was a difficult problem for Chiang to fight against the moral high ground made worse by the fact that his strongest supporters rely on secret police type tools to hunt down the fifth columnists. Two famous intellectuals were assassinated thus losing a lot of Intellectuals sympathies. The popular Warlord of Yunnan Lung was grabbing a lot of attention especially when a Time Magazine article described his bravery on the Salween River Burma. Suddenly a coup was mounted against him and his Army was redeployed to Hanoi Vietnam for the Japanese surrender after which they were sent to fight the Communists in the North where they defected. A brave operation by unknown soldiers smuggled the old Warlord to Hong Kong where he was safe.

Somewhere in the gossip mills I heard a wild rumor. A group of young officers plotted to eliminate corruption of their senior Generals who manipulated the control of supplies and funds. It was by accident that the plot was discovered. An ambitious Intelligence Colonel Chung over heard a tea lady whispering, 'get this message to Wuchang committee.'

He followed the trail back to a newly promoted General. The message was a meeting of Colonels in a code. Wuchang is the famous garrison where the mutiny of 1911 broke out spreading mutiny across the whole nation.

When this situation was discovered the Army executed 16 of the young generals and arrested 600 officers involved in the plot. No action against the corrupt Generals was taken. If the coup succeeded the backbone of the KMT Army would have been broken. Beneath the calm Chungking sky, I never imagined that there were such dangerous developments.

My work in Logistics and Intelligence enabled me to learn of this coup which was partly flamed by the Left Wing Army or Communists presence in Wartime Chungking. After all there was an outwardly harmless Communist Liaison Office in Chungking. There was also a distinct American section of Advisers and Journalists who did not appreciate that a future war between the Communists and Chiang may erupt. They criticized the corrupt KMT Generals badly arousing American public opinions. Even among the American journalists there was the Missionary faction which represented the American Church missions in China which favored Chiang. A Leftist faction is antagonistic towards him.

I learned the hard way that one of the leaders was none other than Colonel Wu my former commander. Silently I prayed for him to escape the hunt for him.

One night it was raining badly when a small number of people knocked at my workshop. Suddenly the door swung open and a dozen gangsters pushed me into a chair.

It was the gangster Boss Yunnan Tung's men armed with machine guns. His lieutenant a man named Yunnan Ma pushed me into a chair and said, 'Will you help us or die with us?'

Major Chan my colleague is part of the Conspiracy for as soon as they broke in, he said, 'Now Colonel Tang it is in such times of emergency that you should forget about your abstract War strategies and help us the real plotters of revolution.'

The tall figure of General Wu walked in followed by Boss Yunnan Kung. He smiled at me but I know that when he smiled weakly he is concealing the truth that he is in serious trouble?

'Are you in serious trouble Sir?' I asked him.

'Life and death matter, Sun Tzu. Have you heard over the radio?'

Boss Yunnan Tung pleaded with me, 'Gary there is a newly assembled plane in the field. Will you give the keys to Walter Kwok so General Wu can escape to Burma?'

The radio announcer's voice on my radio blared out, 'a left wing coup has been uncovered. Our forces are hunting down this traitor General.'

I was left surprised that a fine officer like General Wu could betray us. I looked at him in anger but he said, 'Come now. Sun Tzu states in Chapter 12 that the use of spies is quite a good strategy. Fight for the country but you? you are false Sun Tzu you fight for the private wealth of KMT Generals.'

In exasperation I shouted towards Walter Kwok, 'this man this traitor General saved my life in the Nanjing Battle. Here is your airplane key go to Hell's Angels.'

My deputy Chan took the key and escorted Kwok and Yunnan Tung towards the airplane

At that moment a car screeched outside and three beautiful ladies rushed into my office. I can see Butterfly Ying, and Lucy Wang coming in. Behind them walked Grace Lu but a Grace who is dressed in the uniform of a Colonel of the Leftist Army. There is coldness in her voice as if she is now her real self a professional soldier who worked undercover in the enemy liar.

She saluted General Wu and hugged me.

'We thank you for your help Gary you are a very good friend.'

Was her feeling genuine? I looked at Yunnan Tung who was watching me like a hawk. He too is dressed in the uniform of a Leftist Army Colonel. Somehow his ruthless appearance has softened in the uniform. He smiled apologetically and encouragingly at me.

I mumbled hastily not knowing what to say, 'Go quickly Grace and fly safely.'

Chan escorted them out running quickly, 'quick or you miss the plane.'

Walter Kwok waited until the engine is warm. He told his passengers to brace for the take off. General Wu gave him an order, 'take off without me.'

At that moment a squad of KMT soldiers banged on the door.

Colonel Chung's voice rang out, 'Come out Traitors.'

As soon as the plane took off General Wu put his hands up, 'Hold your fire I surrender.'

I sat down mystified by the spectacle of my ordinary depot being the stage of a spy scandal with the crack anti intelligence chasing the spies. Could Grace the beautiful creature so fashionable and moving with the top army wives be a peasant soldier? I shook my head.

General Wu was put on trial and sentenced to execution. But the Leftist Army approached the KMT General Tang E Bo for a prisoner exchange. But at the height of the negotiations a team of soldiers broke into the prison camp and rescued him. He did escape but 16 Generals and 600 officers were arrested and disappeared from the face of the earth.

I kept in contact with Grace Lu after she settled in Hong Kong. I watched her over the next two years. Perhaps the best evidence is a newspaper cutting from a Hong Kong newspaper which read, 'the Lisa Kung group of high class fashion and jewelry has moved its headquarters from Chungking to Hong Kong. This young woman Grace Lu is one of the richest ladies in Yunnan and Sichuan backed by her husband the Yunnan billionaire.'

Grace wrote to me from Hong Kong, 'I am happy here and free. This island is small but the living is free from wars and fighting.' Grace asked me to tell her whether Yunnan Tung is okay. I promised to check up.

I looked at the face of Chan. He runs our Kunming Depot. 'Let me look at the truck parts storeroom.'

Major Chan said, 'we sent to Chungking 100 trucks assembled this month. Your friend Tung is in danger.'

I spent two hours checking the parts with Chan Reports have come in that Tung's deputy betrayed him and imprisoned him.'

'Chan these two containers, are for my friends, sign the dispatch papers when they come.'

I went to the town centre where Yunnan Tung had a swank hotel but no one knows where he is. Late in the evening I left the bar to go to my room. Grace rang from Hong Kong, 'use the keys I sent you to get into the penthouse. He is imprisoned in the cellar.'

I searched Yunnan Tung's penthouse and found a letter.

'Darling I love you,' signed Lucy Wang.

At that moment a dozen mobsters rushed in and pushed me up badly. Dicey Ma is the new drug lord.

'We meet again,' Yunnan Ma the Dicer looked at me. 'Where is the secret treasure room of Tung?'

Lucy Wang dressed in a smart dress asked, 'I know Grace told you where he hid the treasure chest. Tell us and you can live.'

At that very moment unknown to them, a truck load of foreign soldiers from Burma drove up the Army Stores. Major Chan my deputy looked at them nervously, 'What do you want? Are you not Colonel Kwok?'

'Kwok is my cousin. My Chinese name is Kot. Major Chan, er Uncle I should say, these are orders from Colonel Gary Tang. Here read this.'

'Who are you? You look like his friend Colonel Kwok, no?'

'Look like? He is my cousin your son in law uncle Chan. My Burma name is Colonel Mya Mla of the Burma Border Army,' he turned to his men, 'Men load up the two containers quick. Uncle Chan I believe Gary Tung told you about the containers.'

Chan signed up the dispatch papers. He informed Colonel Mya Mla, 'Tell my friend Colonel Gary Tang that should he have problems in dispatching such a large container to Hong Kong, he should enlist my assistance.'

Meanwhile back at the Penthouse, I asked, 'Dicer Ma, alias Yunnan Ma, you bought Tung's business operations with gold and diamonds, why do you want to steal them back? Grace and Tung need the diamonds and gold for their business in Hong Kong. Where is Yunnan Tung?'

Lucy Wang cried out in a large voice. 'Grace's share is mine. Dicer and I are getting married.'

At that moment Colonel Mya Mla with his men busted into the room. Several of Dicer's men were shot as they resisted.

Yunnan Tung walked in unsteadily helped by a guard. His shirt is untidy and bloody. Colonel Mla said, 'We found him in a cellar tied up. Dicey Ma must be punished.'

Dicey Ma bent on his knees and begged, 'Boss Yunnan Tung please Forgive me, for it was this evil scheming Lucy Wang who tempted me with sex and evil schemes.'

He slapped Wang hard and pleaded 'I promise I will give you a share of my operations.'

Colonel Mya Mla pointed a pistol at his temple. With eyes of anger he spoke in a cold voice, 'the code of the Green Gang to be responsible for your oath of loyalty. You should be shot without mercy Yunnan Ma.'

'Ahh mercy. Boss mercy. Half the takings I promise a thousand times. Mercy.'

Colonel Mla laughed. He walked around the two of them thinking about the offer.

'If you promise half the profits and I will take this woman you call Wang as my concubine.' He held her long hair up and smiled. He thrust her tear filled face to kiss her with a wild kiss.'

Lucy Wang knew her luck had run out. She thought she had learned by twisting her boyfriend Yunnan Ma around that she had made it. But the blood oaths of the Green Gangs is an unwritten law in the wild hills of Yunnan let death be the sentence when a blood oath is broken.

She grabbed this Burmese Chinese soldier and kissed him as seductively as she can. She said, 'if Dicey Ma gives me this poor lady to you, I shall be happy to serve you as your third concubine or fourth concubine. My humble body is yours to serve you day or night, my sweet master. Here another kiss for you my lord.'

Colonel Mya Mla was pleasantly surprised. He nodded at Dicey Ma with pleading eyes.

Yunnan Ma alias Dicey Ma nodded, 'I will never betray you again I promise.' He slapped Lucy Wang and pushed her into Mla's arms, 'here take this pretty lady as your slave here.' He signed the papers put to him by Yunnan Tung.

There was an air of newly found romance in the air as Lucy Wang fussed over the crease on the Colonels uniform and she grabbed his arms around her back. Together they took the lift downstairs.

At the lobby Mya Mla held a quick conference. He said, 'Your friend Major Chan offers to help you and Yunnan Tung. As far as I know he is the Master Courier of the Green Gang in these high mountains. Black gold has been sent to the big cities Shanghai, Guangdong, and Hong Kong by him. We grow the stuff across the border in Burma and send it in packages to Kunming Capital of Yunnan. From Kunming Major Chan takes care of everything. I advise you to see him. Telephone me and tell me where you want your containers to be sent. Okay?'

I turned to Yunnan Tung. 'Sir, Grace Lu requested that I help you and send these gold and jewelry to Hong Kong. What is your instruction?'

Yunnan Tung said, 'twice you have helped me, thanks. I do not think Grace and I are going to be married. There are too many concubines in my wild Hong Kong life. Half the value of the two containers belongs to her and she will sell my share in Hong Kong for me. You take care and bring the stuff to Hong Kong by yourself. Me I am going with Colonel Mya Mla to the opium farms of Burma, His cousin General Walter Kwok send you his best wishes. Goodbye then and take good care of Grace okay?'

I was so tired when I reached Chan's Depot in Kunming. Major Chan welcomed me.

'Welcome Colonel Sir, I have volunteered to help dispatch your two containers to Hong Kong. First here take this.'

I looked at two green letters marked, 'Green Gang Money value 1 million yuans.'

'What is this Chan? '

'As you know I am the front man for the Green Gang in Kunming. The trail of the black gold winds its way downhill to Shanghai and Guangdong. You can go through the city of Guilin in China or since you are going to Hong Kong you should go down south through the city of Hanoi Vietnam. There are bandits at the border with Vietnam. If you or your goods are detained by the local gangs you can pay them through these letters of credit signed by me. They can redeem it at their local banks. There are bandits in the border with Vietnam so only use them sparingly.'

He finished, 'I heard that you shall be transferred to Central China soon congratulations sir. As for annual leave here I have your approved leave for 8 weeks. Come I shall take you to catch the Kunming to Hanoi railway station.'

'What is that? Is there a railway line from Yunnan to Hanoi? I did not know about that?'

Major Chan smiled, 'yes a dangerous but scenic railway line of 890 km built by the French in 1903 for trade with China. In total there are 425 bridges crossing over deep valleys and 155 tunnels, making 36 percent of the total length of Yunnan section. You will disembark at a border town called Hekou and change to a Vietnamese train. But remember the Japanese Army has built a network connecting right up to Burma except for a small stretch near Cambodia. I have written two letters of introduction because the railway was dismantled at a certain section to prevent the Japanese invasion from Vietnam. There will be trucks to take you to Hekou.'

'Well Major Chan thanks anything else?'

Major Chan replied, 'Grace Lu and Yunnan Tung had performed good service for our Green society. Here is a letter of introduction to 14 Pai kou Street, if they are in trouble in Hong Kong tell the local Chieftain to ring me for instructions.'

'Goodbye friend.'

The train journey was calm and peaceful chugging up high mountains and crossing dangerous looking Gorges. I read up on the Vietnam history to prepare myself to proceed from Hanoi to Hong Kong via Macau. The two persons in Vietnamese history who impressed me was a man named Ho Chi Minh and his Deputy a man named Van Giap.

The words stared at me.

'The last time the Chinese came, they stayed a thousand years. The French are foreigners. They are weak. Colonialism is dying. The white man is finished in Asia. But if the Chinese stay now, they will never go. As for me, I prefer to sniff French shit for five years than to eat Chinese shit for the rest of my life.' Ho Chi Minh 1946.

Who is this man Ho Chi Minh? What is he saying is he anti Chinese or anti Christ?'

Can I meet him at all?

Well, when I read the matter further I realize that if I was him I might get just as angry and frustrated as him. Why? Because of International decisions which affects his country's future. The Potsdam Conference countries, namely America, Britain, Russia and China had decided that Vietnam is to be handed to China which will take care of the Northern part and Britain which will take care of the Southern portion. Ho's letters to Roosevelt arguing that his party should take over the whole country had been politely over look, His outburst against this decision came from his heart having been engaged in fighting for the country's independence for many years..

He was speaking at the funeral of a family the family of his Deputy a man named Van Giap, a man who is a fighter and by coincidence a man who studied the works of Sun Tzu's Art of War. The difference between Giap and me is that unlike me he fighting for his life being hunted as a bandit. He is a wanted bandit in Vietnam and he is faced with the War like choice fight back at the French Colonial Government Army with his own Vietnamese Army or is to be hunted and killed like a wild animal. Giap eluded the French Army and the Vietnamese Emperor Bao Dai who was a puppet Emperor stripped off all his powers signed a proclamation to hunt independence fighters. Therefore somehow unbelievably for the French who are famous for their liberal views, the French Colonial Army of Vietnam acted as if it held a divine right to resume its Colonial Government after the Japanese surrender in 1945.

Critics view the French Colonial government as almost exclusively seeking to protect the Catholic religion and Catholic converts in a Buddhist country. They treated the Ngo family like royalty whose members are priests, Bishops, Provincial Governors as well as Interior Ministers in the French colonial administration. Buddhist people were ignored and disadvantaged by this French colonial government staffed by a lot of converts. This rule proved authoritarian, elitist, nepotistic, and corrupt. A Roman Catholic Family the Ngo's were encouraged to rule the country later but it merely continued with the ruling practices of the Colonial government. It pursued biased and religiously oppressive policies against the Republic's natives and Buddhist majority. I can see that the Independence Movements will likely clash against the Catholic convert parties in any future Vietnam change of governments.

Perhaps it is living in the past for the days of Colonialism are over and its time has passed. Yet in 1945 the French Colonial Government returned to Vietnam (Annam and Cochin China) and oppressed the local organizations clamoring for independence. It suppressed the Vietminh movement in the name of poor Bao Dai the helpless Buddhist Emperor who signed proclamations for arrest and executions. Bao Dai was later dethroned by a Catholic Dynasty of Vietnam the famous Ngo brothers. The French officials in 1939 arrested Giap's wife, father in law, sister and young daughter and executed them. Giap was revenge minded later when his Vietminh buried alive a Catholic official from the Ngo family who served the French. Unbelievable for I had heard that in China the top Leftist Commander had his wife arrested and executed in the same way. Somehow I sought evidence that it was the advice of a westerner military adviser from Germany for they were capable of such hatred of the Communists but the only evidence I can find is the scapegoat Bao Dai or decrees of his father Emperor Khai Binh. Later on rightly or wrongly the Viet Minh slaughtered the Officials of the Emperor due to these oppressive policies which had arrested many rebels or their families.

As the train stopped at Hekou a border town I seek help to transfer my cargo to a Vietnamese train. The shopkeeper looked at the letter signed by Major Chan, He telephoned Kunming and told me, 'My name is Peter Dinh, I will personally help clear customs.'

He ordered a truck to transfer the containers to a Vietnamese train bound for Nanning in South China. A French Officer named Captain Jean Lorre asked me some questions.

'Has the cargo of household furniture been inspected?'

Peter answered, 'this is a regular customer from Kunming. Here's the certificate.'

Once on the Vietnamese side I climbed onto the passenger cabin.

The train headed towards Hanoi but at one of the stations it was stopped by a band of bandits.

The bandits went from carriage to carriage calling out names.

'Gary Tang go to the station building.'

There were twelve of us. We stood there facing three leaders of the Bandits.

'We are not bandits but we are the Democratic Republic of Vietnam. Our new country is recognized by the Russians and many International movements.'

He then said, 'you have cargo passing our regional head-quarters therefore you must pay us the taxes. Line up and give us your names.'

I paid them using the Green Gang Paper signed by Major Chan.'

'Very good one million yuan here. Thank you sir. There is a Tea ceremony and a short talk by our leader.'

A wiry man came in. He said, 'Let me introduce you, I am Ho the Chairman, on my right is Giap our Army commander.

Our country is now ruled by the Democratic Party of Vietnam. However the western countries have unjustly divided our country up for foreign colonialists. At the Potsdam Conference they gave Northern half of Vietnam to the Chinese Kuo Min Tang Army. The South of Vietnam they gave the British Army the right to govern. We shall fight for our freedom. We shall drive them out of our country.'

I put up my hands.

'You know Mr. Chairman Yunnan and Vietnam have been friends and traded with each other. In 1946 General Lu Han and his force of 200000 occupied northern Vietnam for six months to takeover from the Japanese surrender. He was a cousin of War-lord Long Yun of Yunnan. I am sure it is a temporary arrangement not a permanent takeover. (General Lu Han changed sides and joined the Communist in 1949) The same temporary administration happened for the British.'

Ho looked sickly and coughed badly. He is known to have tuberculosis in the wild tropical forests.

'I too hope it is temporary but they will give our country to the French not our people.'

General Giap asked, 'you seem to be well known for your views on War Strategy by Sun Tzu. Can a small Army like ours defeat the big Army of the French Army in Vietnam?'

'I am surprised that you have heard about our magazine on Art of War. The Second Sino Japanese War saw the smaller Japanese Army overcome our big Armies. It is not the numbers that count but the thing that matters is War technology and mobility. Surprise is the thing that matters. But the worst war policy is to stand and hold a fort to the last man. We were sitting ducks in a known position and the Japanese knew we were trapped in one position.'

Giap replied, 'Sitting duck well I do hope the French Army will put all their faith in one stronghold, then I shall know how to defeat them soundly. Take the High Ground and pin them down.'

Ho laughed. 'Before you go to China, let us all pray hard for Vietnam to be free one day. Free from the French colonialists.'

Macau and Hong Kong

I miss Grace Lu as a friend but I also miss her as my girlfriend. She is attractive but somehow in her physical presence I feel a bit romantic thinking of her as a marriage partner. It may be my loneliness and lack of girl friends. Grace is so commanding and that everything we decide to do we did together enjoy the happening. Her love of sports is what makes her interesting. We like jogging and going to movies.

When I reached the city of Nanning in China I rang her at the rail station.

In her commanding tone she said, 'Gary I owe you much for this favor. The problem is how to turn the containers into hard bankable cash.'

I suggested 'we ring Major Chan in Kunming if anyone knows he will be the one.'

Grace said, 'look Gary I have many clients in Hong Kong and overseas. There are special auctions for special people. You just store them safely I will get them auctioned off.'

The train reached Guang Zhou station early in the morning. I contacted address given to me and as usual the manager of the shop assured me the goods will be securely stored. That evening I had a wonderful reunion with Grace at one of the many luxurious hotels in the city.

I am so relieved the mission is accomplished. Grace had not been idle I noticed that she was still working for David Kung's mother Liza in an international chain of high value gold and jewelry stores. But she has retired honorably from the service of the Left wing group in Chungking.

Time is short as I had to report for duty.

She thanked me in a special way with some gold presents. 'I have worked hard for Liza Kung and this money may set me up in my own business. It was a dangerous mission you undertook so thanks my friend.'

'Look Grace you are special to me and I am happy to help you. So long as you are happy I shall be happy too.'

Grace kissed me on the lips sweetly which drove me crazy then she said, 'I have arranged a dinner date tonight. I like French food. Will you come?'

I accepted and all day I just thought about her.

That evening we had a fine dinner then we went to a ballroom and danced through the night.

I escorted her to her room and we had after dinner wine.

I took out a box with a gold diamond ring. 'Here Grace my lovely princess would you be my wife make me happy?'

Grace looked surprise. She wore the ring then placed it back. 'Gary I love you very much but you must not propose just like that. I never plan to marry but if I do it will be you.'

'I must confess I am attracted to you Gary.'

I smiled. 'Grace I will propose to you to make you my wife but I knew that you are busy with business. I am just crazy over you and I want you very much. You drive me crazy yearning for you.'

Grace took me in her arms and kissed me tenderly. She laughed. 'Oh you are so old fashioned.'

She took my shirt off and rubbed me hard then led me to her bed.

'Come into my parlor and treat me like a Queen.'

We enjoyed ourselves the whole night and slept deeply. My loneliness has disappeared and I felt a strange bond to this lovely lady called Grace.

The next morning I woke up. She turned towards me, 'Gary I love you too but marry is too big a step. I have a suggestion will you listen?'

I was intrigued. 'Yes I will listen, Grace.'

'Well I love you very much Gary since we met in Nanjing. But when Yunnan Kung left me I vowed I will never marry another man.'

'Yes I am listening. I love you Grace just love.'

'Well Gary maybe we can simply get engaged for a year. No two years. After that if you still want me and I still love you, then I will be your wife.'

I kissed her sweetly as I can. 'Yes I will wait I will wait for sure. You stay in Hong Kong I will come back for you.'

'Give me the ring then.'

'Here Grace will you be engaged to me?' I knelt down. 'Oh yes, by the way, I will also give you a farm which my Dad has in the family if you will be my darling wife.'

She smiled, kissed me then said, 'Yes yes.'

She took the ring.

'Now come to my place in Hong Kong and I will show you a good time.'

I felt lucky. It is like walking in the air to have Grace as my girlfriend. She is beautiful, smart and graceful.

The next 2 weeks I enjoyed myself in post war Hong Kong. Grace worked hard as a Jewelry consultant. She mixed me with a wealthy set of friends such as Harry Kung, his friends one of whom William Koo is quite attracted to Grace. His girlfriend a lady named Meng is quite a well known socialite. I was not too comfortable in this high society set but I enjoyed the drinks and meaningless conversations.

Grace is comfortable but I sensed that deep inside she misses the old way of life in China and the new social divisions in the old society. This girl has a social conscience badly.

One of the films about the new society moved Grace badly. Indirectly it questions the social values of the old China. It is a movie entitled the Goddess which is an old ten year old film from Shanghai. The word Goddess has two meanings it means a mother who is trying to protect her young boy from social ostracism from school friends or it means Shengnu a goddess means a prostitute. The actress Ruan LingYu acted as a poor lady who rents a room from a landlord who steals her life savings. Her boy at school is ostracized because his mother is a prostitute and the community of parents demands the boy be expelled from school. The principal a noble teacher investigates and finds that the boy should not be sacked because it is not his fault but the conservative school sacks the boy and him too. The mother struggles with the landlord who grabs her hidden savings and accidentally she kills him. She is sent to jail, the principal promises to take care of the boy and the Goddess requests him to tell the boy the mother is dead.

Grace cried and cried because this actress Ruan LingYu in real life was exploited by her husband and died killing herself.

The Shanghai press of the day dug up the sadness of her childhood living in abject poverty. They insinuated that she was a kept woman living in a luxury apartment. Relentlessly they dug up the shame of her first husband's rich family rejecting her as a daughter in law because of her servant's background and his squandering her earnings through gambling debts and of her adopted baby. After being hounded in such a cruel way at last she killed herself to the dismay of thousands of female fans It was a double meaning conjuring up her movie role in the film the Goddess Shengnu. Thousands of her fans blocked the Shanghai street traffic for three hours at the funeral of Roan the tragic beautiful actress of Shanghai who died at a young age.

Politically the Communists or Left Wing claimed that many social evils and inequality in society exists which the KMT government as Confucian devils caused by their bribery. Landlords and rich people avoid the justice they deserve. They pointed out the fact there was another child actress who died young. Therefore at the height of the tragedy of Ruan controversy, the Japanese surrendered and civil war between the KMT Army and PLA shook the whole of fabric of society in China. The Left wing critics pointed out that they were the symbols of a new society where justice is doled out without fear or favor. 'If the bad journalists oppress a helpless young actress with dirty exposures, they have broken their oath of office. With the Left Wing in power they will be shot simply without fear or favor, without money and corruption coming in.'

Unaware that they have struck a vital nerve of the womanhood of China in the 1930's and 1940's generation, the Left Wing enjoyed tremendous support from young women who are now educated and intelligent. What sort of future holds for women who live under the Confucian culture? At the most they are employed as ShamShui Nui, women who carry huge loads of sand for concreting in house construction. Most of them work as maid servants in rich households. Majority of them work as prostitutes and vice in the thousands of such establishments. A woman is lucky to be a concubine in rich households serving the rich first sister. From the wilds of the New Women Modern Women romantic dream they heard stories that whilst the Right Wing Confucian Army does not recruit women soldiers the Left Wing Communal Army welcomes women recruit soldiers. Thus, tens of thousands of the women of the 1930's trekked to the jungles to seek their sister soldiers and enrolled. In the Revolutionary Army they found husbands and lived as men and wives. Wild rumors spread about this new way of life and women soldiers became a part of their life. It was like a dream movie where women can fight for justice, join a new world of equality and meet young men with patriotic values who shun corruption. A whole new generation of new China grew in the wild highlands of the western Provinces. It offered escapism in a real world where women suffer from bound feet, working as farm labor or as concubines of the Landlords.

This issue brought Grace and me closer together. I held her hands in mind at the cinema and she held my hands tightly. Though we loved the old China where Confucian rules over the family, yet there are many social ills which Confucian rules caused to women and families. The revulsion of a culture which is foreign to us is forgiven provided it can bring justice back to the people.

Soon we turned our relationship to the raging civil war between the Right Wingers and the Left Wingers. We discussed the war and Grace admitted that she may have abandoned her origins in the country culture by mixing with the rich and famous in Hong Kong who mixed with the top British society in Hong Kong.

As I held her hands and boarded the ship to go to Shanghai I kissed her tenderly and said, 'remember darling, you are my fiancée. I kissed her twice.'

She kissed me gently, smiled weakly, 'You are my fiancée, remember me, well, Gary.'

Hong Kong port was in great confusion as thousands of Shanghai people and businesses fled from Shanghai to Hong Kong for a safe haven. This wave of business migration to Hong Kong in 1947-50 brought much improvement to the local economy.

As my ship floated away from the docks I waved goodbye to Grace, Grace the girl that I loved. She made me feel less lonely and we corresponded well on a large range of topics.

When I reached Shanghai I had time to visit my parents. They were fine My mother told me there were letters and parcels for me. I opened them and saw a big diamond ring.

'Gary I miss you very much. Wear this ring as my fiancée. I love you. Grace.'

chapter

SIX

Last Warlord
Shanxi Wars Central Plains

The Japanese Army targeted the Province of Shanxi as a key state to conquer. Why? It is because of three Strategic reasons. Firstly morally the Warlord of Manchuria in the person of Young Marshall Zhang Xue Liang had been driven out of Mukden (Shenyang) during the 1931 Manchurian Incident. This Army including his younger brother resent the action in keeping him as a hostage or palace prisoner in Nanjing. They defected to the PLA fighting against the Japanese. It is towards Beijing and Shaanxi that his Manchurian Army has retreated to using the old Imperial city of Xi An (ancient Chang An) as its headquarters. Second in history the route of conquest has always been to take Beijing-Hebei then take Central Plains then reach the banks of the Yangzi and take Nanjing and Shanghai. H. Tojo the Commander of the Japanese Kwantung Army laid plans to take Shanxi then threaten Nanjing.

The Japanese under Itagaki Seishiro lost 30000 soldiers but Yan lost 100000 at the bitterly fought Battle of Xinkou. Taiyuan is conquered.

Where's Shanxi? That is the Province which the last Warlord survived in from 1913 to 1949 a continuous period of 36 years. When he finally fled the Province how many of his soldiers die? It was over a hundred thousand casualties or surrenders. Where is Central Plains? The Yellow River winds its way to the East China Sea near Tianjin, and around this river basin is the site of many ancient Chinese Dynasties. Broadly in Shanxi Province lie ancient capitals such as Xian Yang, Xi An, Luoyang, Taiyuan, Zheng Zhou, Kaifeng and Xinxiang. The wartime Communist capital Yenan or Yanan is in Shaanxi a bit due north of Xi An. The Plains bordering the Yellow river are the Central Plains. In the Sino Japanese Wars, the Left Army which grew later to be large enough to be the PLA made a fighting retreat over 12500 km over 13 months called the Long March from Kwangsi (Jiangsi) to the edge of the Central Plains at Yenan in Shaanxi. Nobody knew in 1934 where the retreat was heading as it went towards Sichuan, stopped disappeared then reemerged in Hubei until it finally ended at Yenan which is the west of the Central Plains. In 1947, the Civil War was refought after the Japanese surrender in 1945. The KMT Army deployed an Army of 3 million men to encircle the PLA then finish it off once encircled. But half is stationed at Manchuria near the Soviet and North Korean border. The main force lay at Wuhan which is closest to Yenan but when the Manchurian fronts opened up it shifted to the central plains. But there is a force at Shanxi of 200000 belonging to the Warlord of Shanxi Yan Shi Shan. He had changed flags and is under the direction of the KMT Central command. In theory this force is of strategic value because it cuts off escape from Yenan.

How big is the foe's force? The big surprise is that when the KMT Army attacked and drove into Yenan it was found evacuated to nil. Where can they be in 1947?

Their mobility is remarkable one day they feint and is there next day they feint and they are gone. If they had fought to the last man they can be proud but dead men.

The KMT Army by 1948 is in a defensive position with its aim to prevent the foe from crossing the Yangzi river to advance into

Shanghai. Their Army in the far north theatre in Manchuria had been pinned down. In the Liao Sheng or Manchurian War zone they had lost and in the Pingjin Campaign they were mauled. In the central plains south is the city of XuZhou (not SuZhou) with Liu Chih in nominal command but three key Generals named Huang, Qiu and Du in support roles. The numbers were 900000 men KMT and 600000 men PLA. Huang's division suffered defections of 23000 leaving him trapped with 50000 men. Qiu was ordered but failed to relieve him and Huang fell. Later Qiu was ambushed and he too fell. Their chief Du tried to break out but was captured.

With 900000 men lost or defected what is to be done? Should they fight to the last man like Huang and Qiu or be captured like Du or survive to fight another day? This question laid on the minds of this old Warlord Yan Shi Shan who is well experienced in survival against all odds.

Warlords are peculiar to an age in the last decade of the 19th century. It was a time of flux when Confucian society resisted change but the world left the old Confucian rules of blind absolute obedience behind. The country underwent great changes in politics and military affairs as the Japanese Army grew in strength. These old Warlords were swept away because they failed in Defense and left the country swinging under a Japanese pendulum.

Yan Shi Shan born 1883 was a small time Warlord in Shanxi in 1913 but he was the last Warlord who died (1960).

For me in a year later after Hong Kong in 1947, I was in the Chinese civil war. 'The Central Plains lay between the hilly ancient imperial cities such as Xianyang, its twin city Xi An (Shanxi), eastwards to Luo Yang northwards to Taiyuan, Luo Yang eastwards to Zheng Zhou, Kai feng then to the Shandong province.'

As the central plains in history was the scene of many wars which gave rise to new dynasties it would be interesting to know that dynasties and tyrant Emperors such as Yang Ti of Sui Dynasty fought crucial wars in these Plains. The Tang Dynasty followed the Sui Dynasty and the Great Emperor Li Shih Min in 618 was Commander in wars against the Tartars as well as rival Princes skirting the Central Plains.

In ancient days there were no cinemas but the Chinese Opera came to town annually at the Spring Harvest festival. Half a days work and an opera stage is ready to perform. Operas were played at the Emperors' court and at every place where there is a village green.

The soft sing song voice of narrator at the Open Air theatre mounted on a platform went on, 'Here are these ancient battlefields of the Sui Dynasty and battles refought later in the Tang dynasty.'

With a clang and cymbal he waved his hands in a sweeping motion then walked to the centre stage.

'Look at the green hills and small rivers the innocent scene of country life is interrupted by wild wars between city states. The fall of the Northern Wei Dynasty ushered in the usurper Yang Jian who fought rival generals until he became the Emperor Wen first emperor Sui Dynasty in 581. Here, rode the Armies of Yang Guang (later Sui Yang Ti) his son of sons the last Sui Emperor who was ambitious to be Emperor after his father Emperor Wen. He arranged the dethronement of the Crown Prince his elder brother Yang Yong in 600 and in 604 he prevented the reappointment of Yang Yong by killing him. His father Emperor Wen being ill at the summer palace heard that he tried to seduce Consort Chen at the summer palace and ordered two ministers to summon Yang Yong for re enthronement. Yang Guang still crown prince arrested the two high officials. But an assassin Zhang Heng employed by Yang Guang (Emperor Sui Yang Ti) finished the Emperor Wen leaving Sui Yang Ti to become the new Emperor. Later Cheng Heng the officer who killed Emperor Wen as he lay ill at his summer palace was himself marched towards the execution ground. At his execution he lamented why he had done favors for this Crown Prince which went unrewarded. This Crown Prince later made them his concubines the young consorts Chen and Cai from his father's Palace Household. Those were blood thirsty years with the father General Wen in his hey days in 585 destroying many enemies of the Northern Wei dynasty. The son Sui Yang Ti in 618 faced over 9 rebellions caused by his expensive foreign wars which bankrupted the poor peasants. He went mad awaiting his own fate. Afraid of his wrath and fearing a sudden order to execute them his own Generals took his life. General Yuwen

Huaji killed Sui Yang Ti crowned him self but he was later killed by another General named Wang.

Yang Ti's reign brought bankruptcy to the country as he sent a 300000 army to attack Goryneo and many other wars.

History books of that time record that his father Emperor Wen of the Sui Dynasty summoned the elder brother intending to re appoint him as Crown Prince. The act was prompted by then crown prince Sui Yang Ti's attempted molesting of the young queen Consort Chen and Consort Cai while his father was ill. He became a tyrant Emperor wasting the country's wealth on foreign wars until taxes were so heavy the country rebelled. Thus, end the days, of Sui Yang Ti.'

Many scholars argue that Sui Yang Ti was a good emperor who expanded the frontiers. But others argue that he was a tyrant who killed his own father. It is not for me to question but simply enjoy the show. As a Warlord Sui Yang Ti was a ruthless commander.

With the drama hot up, a female narrator danced onto the stage to tell of the Tang dynasty. Her shrill voice in the 1947 night air somewhere in the war time city of Taiyuan in Shanxi thrilled the small audience who listened enraptured. Many in the audience are soldiers of KMT Army as allies of the old Shanxi Warlord Yan Shi Shan including my friend Lieutenant Colonel Chung and me.

As young men we knew that in 1930 Warlord Yan and the Warlord Feng Yu xiang with his large army the Guominjun had fought the Central Plains War against Chiang's KMT Army as it tried to advance on Beijing. Somehow Yan Shi Shan changed flags and occupied Beijing in 1931 as ally of Chiang's KMT government. Young Marshall Zhang son of the late Fengtian (Mukden) Warlord Zhang Tso Lin of Manchuria was overall Warlord in these regions. Those were the days when the Japanese Kwangtung Army in Manchuria were planning to bring the former child emperor of China Pu Yi into Manchuria and proclaiming him in 1932 Emperor of Manchukuo a new independent state.

The League of Nations appointed the Lytton Commission which condemned it but the Japanese Army in China simply resigned from the League. This old grudge was up in the air and the western allies fighting against Japan in the World War 2, planned to renew the issue through war.

There followed the 1931 Mukden Incident in which quietly without a fight the Manchurian Army escaped to Shanxi and Young Marshall Zhang Xue Liang changed its flag to become Chiang's North Eastern Army.

Who you may ask is this Warlord Yan Shi Shan? He is an old Warlord the last Warlord from the days of Warlord of Warlords Yuan Shih Kai. After the 1911 XinHai rebellion which overthrew the Manchu Dynasty Yuan's military took over appointing civilian Ministers in the manner of the ancient emperors. This alienated the KMT and Democratic parties who demanded elections. In his youth (born 1883-1960) Yan was military student in Japan who joined Sun Yat San at the same time in 1908 as Chiang (1887-1975). Posted to Shanxi as Division Commander around 1909 he joined the 1911 Revolution becoming a Warlord of Shanxi. In 1913 Warlord Yuan Shih Kai grabbed military power from the Rebel Movements headed by Sun Yat San. He assassinated Sun's key supporters such as Song Ji Ren and Chiang Kai Shek's military mentor Chen Q M.

In one stroke China changed from a Democratic Republic to a Dictator controlled Republic. Many patriotic people were killed but all that Sun Yat San could do is flee to Japan.

Warlord Yan changed flags to be under Yuan and personally controlled Shanxi for many years. Yan to us and many other men is a survivor. He never fights a stronger foe like the Japanese, or Yuan Shih Kai but will surrender and survive with gifts, flattery and favors including getting rid of unwanted rivals. His friend Warlord Feng Yu Xiang is famous for betrayal. An ally, of Chi Li clique of Warlords under Wu Pei Fuh. Wu planned an ambush of the Fengtian clique soldiers at the Shanhai Pass but suddenly Feng his ally at the rear staged a coup taking Beijing. Wu the famous strategist fled badly defeated.

Colonel Chung said, 'hush lets see the end of the Opera.'

I replied, 'come on this is not real opera must be one of the many left wing modern operas sprouting all over the countryside.'

'No,' Chung replied, 'after tonight they will stage the famous opera Drunken Beauty Yang Kui Fei betrayed by the Emperor for another getting drunk. You don't expect top stars like Mei Lan Fang to perform in this village square do you?''

At this stage our Opera conversations were interrupted by the restarting of the Open Air Chinese Opera theatre.

The shrill voice of the opera narrator rang out.

'The Sui Dynasty did not last long. The next Dynasty the Tang Dynasty occupied the same countryside of the rolling hills in this region. Down here in 618 rode the victorious Li Shih Min known as Emperor Taizhong who assisted his father General Li Yuan to become the emperor after the fall of the Sui Dynasty. Nine rebellions raged through the land but Li Yuan a famous Sui General fought the rebellions. The same family assassinations of the Sui Emperors took place with the Li rulers of Tang Dynasty.

In summer 618, when news came at Chang An Emperor Sui Yang Ti had been killed at Jiangdu by General Yuwen Huaji, Li Yuan (Emperor Gaozu) at Chang An who was holding Emperor Gong made him abdicate the Sui throne to him as Emperor Gaozu of Tang dynasty. He created eldest son Li Jian Cheng as crown prince and second son Li Shih Min the Prince of Qin and army commander.

Something in the culture of ancient kings makes mutual jealousy at the court of Emperor Gaozu a deadly tradition. If left unrestrained it became a struggle for power flamed by court advisers. Li Shih Min was sent to several key battles which he won with glory. One peasant rebel named Dou crowned himself King of Xia. In a battle at Luo Yang a rebel General Wang was besieged at Luo Yang but requested help from Dou, king of Xia who agreed to send a strong Army to resist Li Shih Min.

Li Shih Min left a small detachment, at Luoyang, but staged a surprise to ambush King Dou at Hulao Pass. Li Shih Min defeated Dou and captured him. A force of 1000 elite Guards dressed in black highly skilled at Bow and Arrows killed the soldiers of Dou at Hulao (Tiger) Pass. He took Dou back to Luoyang and displayed him for execution.

Li Jian Cheng, the Crown Prince was jealous of the victories of Li Shih Min. He was instigated by advisers to plot the downfall of Li Shih Min. When he and 3rd brother, Li Yuan Ji persuaded the

Emperor Gaozu to appoint Yuan Ji in replacement as Army commander to fight a foreign war Li Shih Min's advisers warned him that he is under great danger from them.

'If before he becomes Emperor he treats you with suspicion then after he becomes Emperor he treats you with execution.'

Emperor Gaozu did not depose Li Jian Cheng as Crown Prince as promised to second son Shih Min, who complied with task to put down rebellion by first son's commander named Wang. Li Shih Min suffered another danger when Gaozu was persuaded to sack his three closest advisers whose martial skills are invaluable.

After a banquet at Li Jian cheng's palace Li Shi min fell into a food poisoning scare. It was an assassination attempt.

Zhangsun Wuji suggested, 'we attack first Li Jian Cheng and Li Yuanji.' Li Jian Cheng persuaded Emperor Gaozu to remove Fang and Du, as well as Li Shih Min's trusted guard officers Yuchi Jingde and Cheng Zhijie, from Li Shih Min's staff. Zhangsun Wuji, who remained on Li Shih Min's staff, continued to try to persuade Li Shih Min to attack first.

Li Shih Min, who believed that with the army in 3rd brother Li Yuanji's hands, the final coup is made and he would be attacked so he moved first. Li Shih min accused Li Jian Cheng and Li Yuanji of committing adultery with Emperor Gaozu's concubines. Emperor Gaozu, summoned both to answer. As the first Prince Li Jian Cheng and third Prince Li Yuanji approached the central gate leading to Emperor Gaozu's palace, the Xuanwu Gate, Li Shih min the second Prince stood on the roof in black uniform and a black hood. He aimed and fired an arrow that hit first Prince the Crown Prince Li Jian cheng. Li Jian Cheng turned to run mortally hurt but Shih min leapt from the roof with a sword and finished the evil plotting and private rivalry against him. Yuchi jumped hidden from the roof and attacked third Prince Li Yuanji. Yuan Ji was a great fighter and parried the sword attack but when he turned to run into the garden Yuchi struck him in the head.

It was the signal for a coup as Li's soldiers appeared around the small band of the late Crown Prince.

Li Shih Min's forces surrounded the palace in a coup and demanded Emperor Gaozu (566-635) in 628 aged 62 to agree to create Li Shih min crown prince. Li Jian cheng's and Li Yuanji's sons were killed, and Li Shih Min took Li Yuanji's wife Princess Yang as a concubine. Two months later, Li Shi Min demanded and Emperor Gaozu yielded the throne to him for reasons unknown but Gaozu's courtiers especially Feng De Yi a Chancellor was loyal to Gaozu and seen to be playing both sides. Thus Li Shih Min became Emperor Tai Zhong co founder Tang dynasty.

He is typically considered one of the greatest, if not the greatest, emperors in Chinese history. It was in these parts of China where ancient capitals like Chang An (Xi An) Taiyuan Luo Yang, Zheng Zhou, that battles were fought.

Site of ancient battlefields
Now in 1947 the old battlegrounds will see battles of the civil war between the Communist Army renamed PLA and the KMT Army being refought.

Who I asked again is this Warlord Yan Shi Shan? Whilst the KMT Army was driven to Chungking, Yan ruled Shanxi centered at Taiyuan. In a bitter battle of Xinkou in 1937 the famous Itagaki Divisions suffered heavy losses 30000 dead, 30000 wounded before capturing Xinkou. Yan lost 90% of his Army. Till 1945, the Japanese Army controlled the towns but the countryside was controlled by the PLA and to a lesser extent Yan.

Yan during war years played both sides being friendly with the Left Army against the Japanese who occupied Taiyuan, but an ally of the KMT Army. Shanxi was east of Shaanxi where the Left Army was believed to be sited. With encirclement in the minds of the KMT Commander, the Shanxi Army of Warlord Yan in 1947 was built up to 140000 men plus a mercenary army of 12000 surrendered Japanese ex soldiers. The Left Army now renamed the PLA no longer trusted Yan as an ally and caused a large number of desertions from his army. Their central Army headed by a famous one eyed General named Liu stayed hidden somewhere between the Song Mountains and Huai river avoiding ambush but ready to counterattack.

Now in 1947, the civil war consisted of three stages. Firstly, control of Far Northern Manchuria zone including capital of

Beijing. Liao Shen means Liaoyang and Shenyang (old name Mukden). Second the mid northern zone consisting of the central plains, Song mountains and Huai river and Shanxi. Third is the frontline zone. This comprises the Yangzi river zone including Wuhan, Nanjing and Shanghai facing Yenan in Shaanxi. Somewhere in the war years the old concept of encirclement of the Communists Guerrillas had unknown to the KMT undergone much change. The small band guerillas have grown to be full Armies.

The hunted guerrillas had become a Peoples Army with a capacity to fight a battle of counter encirclement. We the encirclement army may become the encircled. The thought never reached the minds of Yan and his war planners. Meanwhile the rate of surrenders of Yan's and the KMT Army continued to rise due to the bad image of corruption of the unpopular government. Several runaway inflations countrywide increased the disaffection of the country population. With economic problems Yan's Army of 200000 needed increased funding but corruption deprived much war equipment. Does he have to rely on the old Infantry Strategy of fighting to the last man?

Yan was a controversial Commander who requested the Japanese Army in his Province of Shanxi in 1945 to surrender to him, and then re engage them as mercenary soldiers under his command. This suggestion was opposed by the surrendered Army Command in Japan and the Americans but he sidestepped the issue by asking them to resign from the Army before engaging them again. A total of 12000 to 5000 signed up and took part in the Defense of Shandang and Taiyuan.

Battle of Shandang South Shanxi

This Battle in October 1945 was aimed at driving the Left Wing Army later the PLA from southern Shanxi which borders Shaanxi and Yenan. The PLA strength was estimated to be less than Yan's Army of 35000. General She Ze Bo drove into the area and controlled a southern city ZhengZhi. But he was surrounded and a siege took place. Meanwhile the PLA encircled the city but could not take it suffering big losses. They then set out on a tricky tactic making the Yan Generals think that they had cornered their foes. Yan sent in a second Commander Peng Yu Bin to reinforce General She. At first Peng managed to inflict heavy losses but then he fell into the trap of pursuing the enemy regiments deep into the hills. Suddenly he encountered fire from ambush and was trapped. He lost the battle fighting to the last man. Peng died in the ambush. The PLA then attacked in force and General She's fort was overrun. He was captured giving the foe control of Southern Shanxi. .

Two key Generals fell into traps one Peng Yubin died and one She ZeBo was captured, while pursuing the PLA. They were the pursuers who became ambushed and encircled. A third Army at the Tiger Pass was wiped out.

Yan in 1947 controlled Shanxi facing Shaanxi a strategic position of encirclement. In two key battles he lost Shandang in 1946 and Taiyuan in late 1948 even though he had a paid ex Japanese Army veterans numbering 12000 plus his regulars.

Battle of Taiyuan North Shanxi

By 1947 Yan's control of Shanxi was restricted to Taiyuan his capital city for 36 years. Yan knew that the Communists were growing stronger, and would rule half of China. Would his battle strategy involve a stand to the last man?

There was a small chance that the Americans may step in to rescue him. If so it would be worthwhile to make a stand to the last man. But in common with the general feeling in the whole country as well as in America there was excessive corruption or misuse of power at the expense of the Aid Donor country. Therefore the Americans prepared to assist Chiang by evacuation to Taiwan. The Americans definitely prefer to assist Chiang as their Ally in preference to any other Chinese leader. For example in 1948 Chiang was forced after a great defeat to resign as President and Li Zong Zen acted as President with Yan as Prime Minister. But Chiang withheld aid of 250 million from Li. In the end Chiang regained the position of President after the retreat to Taiwan.

Taiyuan is in the foothills near the Great Wall of China. The capture of Taiyuan is important to the Left Wing Army because Yan is a crafty Commander who may arrange a major reinforcement and counter attack. Symbolically as the last Warlord still involved in War, if he is driven out and retreats south, the PLA will have full control of North China. In the past he had hidden in the hills and came back later in a crafty manner. A morale and psychological victory is at stake.

Yan knew he was surrounded by territory controlled by the Communists. An assault on Taiyuan is expected so he prepared his armies by fortifying over 5,000 bunkers, constructed over the rugged terrain surrounding Taiyuan. The Nationalist 30th Army was airlifted from Xian to Taiyuan to fortify the city, which was protected by over six hundred pieces of artillery. Yan repeatedly declared his intention to die in the city in the Battle of Taiyuan. The total number of KMT soldiers by the fall of 1948 was 145,000.

As the clock ticked in November 1948 Chiang made preparations to retreat to Taiwan. The PLA encircled Taiyuan and captured the outer ring of defenses with hard fought battles. A Yan General tricked the PLA he would surrender then arrested the officer who came to accept the surrender who was executed. But this Officer was later captured and executed in revenge. For many months the defense of Taiyuan held out. But suddenly the Leftist Army was victorious in neighboring Hebei Province and their numbers increased to 320000.

Yan's commander of military police force Sun Chu and son-in-law, Wang Jingguo, in charge of most Nationalist forces was ready to fight to the last man. Overall command was delegated to Imamura Hosaku, the Japanese lieutenant-general who had joined Yan after World War II. This General later committed suicide when the city fell.

In 1949 the outlying defense posts had been captured and a call for surrender was made but it was rejected by Yan. On April 22, 1949, the Communists bombarded Taiyuan with 1,300 pieces of artillery and breached the city's walls. Bloody street-to-street fighting for control of the city ended with defeat or Yan. The Taiyuan Campaign ended with many Nationalist officers committing suicide when the city fell. The dead included Yan's nephew-in-law, serving as governor, and his cousin, who ran his household. Yan's remaining forces and those of the warlord's thousands of Japanese mercenaries surrendered giving the foe complete control of Shanxi.

As he left Taiyuan by air, to fly to Nanjing, defeat is in the air though he used the term going to plead for new reinforcements and supplies. Survival, a concern for personal survival had always saved him in hard times.

Am I sad or happy?

If I can equate Yan to our notorious Warlord Yuan Shih Kai, then I am happy that this Warlord has become obsolete in War strategy.

Yan Shi Shan as the last Warlord of China fought for his personal survival through most of his career playing up to and flattering his superiors. As for me I have always wanted some one with power to get rid of Warlords forever. They have been cruel, corrupt and played their country out to foreign powers in particular during the Sino Japanese Wars.

As for the loss of lives of brave Army officers who prefer to die for their country rather than surrender their personal values, this is my major criticism, 'live to fight another day and survive to fight another way.' A battle may be lost but the war must be won.

It is truly an ancient and obsolete standard of War strategy to order stand to the last man, to prove that as a soldier we are brave. It is more fruitful to aim for final victory of your army rather than to battle over a certain outpost.

That reminds me of a man I met in Vietnam back in 1940's. Van Giap in the Battle of Dien Bien Phu, saw that the French Colonial Army had selected a fixed position in a jungle fort to fight to the last man. Van Giap use artillery, mobility and destruction of their air strip to prevent reinforcement. He was the first Asian General to win a victory over the western nations. It made me very happy to explain Sun Tzu's War strategy using this example set up by this man named General Giap. The French General in charge of artillery Defence admitted it was his fault for under estimating Giap then he shot himself. I was surprised that there are, western generals who commit suicide on losing a battle.

As for the Sino Japanese Wars the point I remember is that a victory is complete only when the enemy leader's head is captured. Chiang was never captured in the Sino Japanese Wars and remained in the war fighting back.

China where it all began

When Japan surrendered in 1945 the puppet Prime Minister Wang Jing Wei fled to Japan where he died in mysterious circumstances. He was a great traitor unaware that he was holding himself to be a true Confucian Gentry man.

As for the Japanese Army in China after the surrender they were disarmed. What happened to the Japanese Army Generals after the World War 2 surrender? There was held War Crimes Tribunal in Tokyo where 28 were charged with War Crimes A, and 5700 charged with War Crimes B or C. In China the War Crimes Tribunal charged over 500 cases. Surrendered soldiers were repatriated to Japan.

A second repercussion of the War was the Post War Reconstruction program in which industries were developed. Surprisingly new Electrical Companies were founded such as Akio Morita of Sony, H Matsushita, and Sanyo which became world leaders in consumer goods. Honda and Toyota and Mitsubishi became leaders in the car industry. However complaints against the poor quality of Japanese goods spurred the industry to engage in quality control and product research.

The government was again returned to the civilian Cabinets. Another controversial clause involved the aversion to future war and restriction from organizing an Army except for self defense.

One controversial issue was the formation of a body to organize comfort women for the occupying army. It was not certain why but skeptic writers pointed out that the ancient fear that a conquering army may engage in barbaric practices against women and families as did their army in the war may have an influence on the thinking of these organizers.

Back in China, the Nationalist government returned in triumph to Beijing and Nanjing in 1946 but unknown to us a great civil war was being fought. The claim to hold Beijing eluded the Kuo Min Tang government because the countryside surrounding Beijing in the provinces of Hebei, Henan, Shanxi, and Manchuria were controlled by the PLA. It would be dangerous to station troops in cities of these regions because the guerrilla army of the PLA may launch surprise attacks on or capture the garrisons in these regions.

There were four theatres of war. First the Yangzi zone directed at encirclement of the red headquarters at Yenan. The Central Plains theatre at Shanxi is near the Song mountains and Huai river. Third the Beijing Tianjin Hebei zone theatre of war. Fourth the Manchurian zone theatre, at Shenyang (Mukden) and Chang Chun the capital. The foe was the Leftist Army under its inspirational Commander and Prime Minister Zhou a quiet man who inspired millions in history. Later he reconciled with America striking a middle path.

In Manchuria the Russians disarmed the Japanese Army and handed much war equipment to the Leftist Army. In response the Japanese Army surrendered to the KMT and handed much equipment to them. A terrible civil war was begun which did not end until 1949. It was history repeating itself as I saw the KMT Army with half a million men taking over the old Japanese Army cities such as Changchun, Mukden, the Jehol areas. There was one great weakness the Nationalist KMT Armies had to be airlifted by air because the PLA controlled the central plains. This was an advantage rapid deployment but also a disadvantage no ground control. Many of our Sun Tzu group felt that fighting slowly up north is better than sitting in strange cities being totally surrounded.

The Communist Armies renamed PLA enjoyed better mobility and captured the KMT General Du Yuming. I knew Du was a professional soldier whose loyalty to Chiang is never questioned. His most famous victory was disarming the Yunnan Warlord at Kunming and sending him to Chungking.

But was this an action that engendered loyalty to Du or his Boss Chiang? No because Long Yun's Commander a General named Zeng felt guilty and sorry for his superior for being unable to save his Warlord from dismissal. He was one of a dozen defections. The personal loyalty of a General towards his War Lord had been violated but he suffered the shame in silence. And so now in 1947 9 years later he found himself defending Chang Chun the vital frontline at JinZhou had been taken after a ferocious battle. At the critical battle for the Manchurian capital of Chang Chun the former Yunnan Army General Zeng surrendered to the Peoples Liberation Army dealing a serious and fatal blow to Chiang's Army of nearly a million men in Manchuria centered at Shenyang (formerly Mukden).

Was General Du Yuming the man at Shengyang (Mukden) able to match the Communist Generals in Manchuria after his superior Chen Cheng was defeated and encircled? His predecessor Wei Li Kuang lost key cities like Jinzou in close fighting. Du was given a hard task. He already controlled the cities but the enemy forces were elusive and moves quickly. To defeat them you need to know where they are and then hunt them down.

He fought on till encircled and was tamely captured perhaps not expecting a victory and not with fire and zeal. Our study group a secret society for the study of Sun Tzu's War strategy, debated the issue in secret in the old school hall at Shenyang.

I told the small audience of officers comprising generals, Colonels, Captains and Sergeants, 'The vote is close very close. Our Army will have to be defeated for three reasons. First an Army of half a million airlifted into Manchuria is like a fortress swimming among the sharks in the stormy seas. If any troubles arise, there will be no reinforcements to call on. Second the ratio of superiority was ten to one that means the Leftist Army of yesterday should be 50000 but that is no longer true. Their army now at half million we need a 5 million men Army to let the ratio stand. Thirdly the oath of loyalty and fighting spirit among Sun Tzu Generals is sadly lacking in our Army. If Shenyang falls the neighboring Divisions will not come to its aid because they will not survive the exercise. It is partly due to petty jealousy but mainly self survival.'

One of the Generals shouted, 'According to Sun Tzu we stand or fall together. We must fight as one united country.'

This officer was implying that the fault lay with the leader of leaders. I shouted at him, 'according to Sun Tzu you can be praised if the High Command likes it but you can be shot if they feel you are disobedient.'

He persisted, 'that was not taught at military school, never.'

We all remained silent for there are things we can and cannot, say, or do.

Chen Cheng had commanded major battles of the Sino Japanese Wars but made an error disbanding the Manchukuo soldiers numbering 1.2 million instead of retraining them. In 1946 the Left wing Army had become a Communist Liberation Army which had barely survived for many years running from the Japanese Army who hunted them. But now in 1946 they were experienced and equal to the KMT Army in Manchuria. For once in their battle history they were prepared to fight a head on traditional battle. With so much at stake, they were very careful making sure the Railway was under their control thus denying the KMT Army from reinforcements.

I assembled on a board the two KMT and PLA armies facing each other in Manchuria. The PLA controlled the railway and encircled the KMT Army. From this I announced to my fellow military study groups that the hunter has become the hunted thoroughly encircled. In the past the KMT Army hunted the PLA units who hid in the remote hills. But PLA had adopted the Japanese tactic encircle then finish the besieged city.

According to Sun Tzu's strategy the PLA Army had spent 11 years hiding from the Nationalist Army's superior firepower in order to survive in the wild hills. Thus when Du Yuming and Chen Cheng the great Nationalist General were sent to Manchuria to fight the Communists they did not realize it was a different war. The PLA which they used to encircle and hunted down, are now well armed, with great mobility and expert in using feints and deceptions and all out attacks.

The practice of retreating or evading from direct battles was like second nature to them no pride just survival to fight another day but the Nationalist Generals are fatalistic willing to stand to the last man. Their armies started with superior forces but were counter encircled time and again until they were forced to retreat south back to Shanghai and Su Zhou. Hence Du was not able to fight a foe which was able to move fast, a foe which was expert at ambush and encirclement and most important when their chips are down they value escaping for Survival to fight another day. But the Nationalists fought to the last men refusing to fight another day. Some brave Generals lost their lives by suicide.

Reluctantly our study group which operates like a secret society of Sun Tzu's Art of War spread the word that Manchuria cannot be held.

Last Warlord

Yan Shi Shan loved his position as Warlord of Shanxi so much he started a front at Taiyuan with 146000 men. Somehow he persuaded the National Treasury to bankroll his mercenary Army of 12000 ex Japanese soldiers in the old Warlord belief that Japanese soldiers fight better. He tried to reassert control over his home province of Shanxi, but found like the Japanese that he could control the cities but not the countryside. But the PLA is a new type of foe which encircled his capital at Taiyuan. Yan was at Shanxi east of Yenan the Communist headquarters. They encircled Yenan but found that the troops were not there. Suddenly the communists laid a siege on Taiyuan. Fighting was fierce and Taiyuan was captured after losing 70000 soldiers but the Nationalist Garrison was wiped out 140000 killed or captured. Yan the old Warlord made preparations to fly to Taiwan accepting the fact he had lost the civil war.

Where did the red troops go when the KMT took their headquarters at Yenan? The KMT military commanders such as Chen Cheng, Du Yuming, Li Zong ren, now faced a foe which had gained experience evading the attacks of the Japanese Army for 11 years. They found that occupation of key Manchurian cities was not wise in the presence of an enemy Army which disappears in the day. It was risky and vulnerable to encirclements. Encircled they were and many KMT Generals when encircled were persuaded to defect or change sides instead of fighting to the last man.

When key Generals such as Wei Li Huang, Du YuMing, Chen Cheng and also the Warlord Yan, lost their campaigns the possibility of defeat began to be considered. Attempts to retreat were cut off and several brave Generals fought to the last in the river Huai campaigns. Reluctantly they fled back to the mid south after two key and elite fighting divisions were defeated.

History repeats itself when after the victories in the former Manchuria battles the Left Wing Army or PLA advanced on Shanghai and Nanjing. Only difference is this time it is the PLA which advanced south not the Japanese Army in China.

When Chiang's army retreated to the island of Taiwan the new PLA Army proclaimed the new Peoples Republic. In the North Eastern war theatre the KMT Armies, were captured or surrendered.

Advance and Retreat. Surprise Ambush

As the civil war raged on, I was sent to the central plains on an encirclement mission. There we encountered this strange war strategy. We encircled the band of 10000 men who sought to escape to the river. We caught them at the rivers edge and they stood to fight. For an hour we called in air bombers. Just as we started to charge their position, we heard several bugle calls. Suddenly at our flank there were 10000 soldiers and another 15000 soldiers to our back. Their infantry charged at us outnumbered by 10000 men. Without tanks and artillery support it was the same infantry war which I had fought for 20 years. Our frontline ran and we were captured.

I was exhausted but then I saw their Commander walk into our pen and looked straight into my eyes.

'Ha, Colonel Tang,' he laughed, 'are you still the Sun Tzu Art of War adviser of old?'

I laughed humbly and I retorted, 'Ha Major Wu err sorry General Wu, so this is your art of War, Retreat when Sun Tzu advances, Harass us when we pause, then Attack us when we retreat.

Deception means a sham a fraud and dishonest twisting of the truth. It all started when our Command was told that a 5000 band of bandit rebels is hiding in the hills. With 20000 men we surrounded them pursuing them as they fled. After three days we were exhausted and stopped to rest but they showed their hands and shot at us. Without rest and tired we fought back and cornered them at the river crossing. Suddenly new bandits attacked us from the flank 10000 of them and from our rear another 15000. We the hunter became the hunted as their fresh bandits with force charged at us yelling wildly. Our men panicked broke rank and fled at the frontline giving the Bandits the victory. I realized too late that it was a deception right from the start and we are entrapped.

Quietly I began to feel that the KMT Army did not have the internal unity of command that is crucial in a War. Their Generals were a loose federation of cliques and inner circles. Once shattered the cliques only concern their selves with survival not a battle. It is a Classical caricature of Yuan Shih Kai the King of cliques? Will we lose the civil war? I despair when I realize that a clique network is not suited for a life and death battle but ideal for survival of a defection inclined General.

Internal strength

What is inner strength and what has the Japanese Generals got that gave them inner strength? Is it Bushido?

In Chinese Generals what is inner strength? In times of War, the swearing of oaths by Generals or secret society leaders towards each other creates strong bonds of life and death. In contrast some weaker minded secret society leaders break their oaths secretly and betray their brothers.

An analogy can be taken from the corrupt Generals. They engage in corrupt conduct protecting their own cliques no matter what oath. In contrast some sources say the Communist Generals swore oaths which are more truly about mutual survival. As bandits they were hunted down and to survive their need for each other were genuine. I read and reread the ancient classic all men are brothers. They too were hunted as bandits and later emerged as emperors men.

The ancient oath sworn in the Peach Garden by Liu Bei, Zhang Fei, and Guan Yu was described in The Romance of the Three Kingdoms. It stressed the loyalty to one's sworn brothers and commitment to righteousness (Yi):

We three, Liu Bei, Guan Yu and Zhang Fei, though of different families, swear brotherhood, and promise mutual help to one end. We will rescue each other in difficulty, and we will aid each other in danger. We swear to serve the state and save the people. We ask not the same day of birth, but we seek to die together. If we turn aside from righteousness or forget kindliness may Heaven and man smite us!

All the onlookers did not appreciate the wry humor which I had. But General Wu the one eyed former Major Wu laughed.

'Ha Colonel Gary Tang you are still talking Sun Tzu when you are captured.'

Then he said, 'we travel light cannot take prisoners. If these were ancient times surely we would kill all but if you swear not to fight us again we will leave you. Good bye.'

As soon as he spoke the sound of a relief column approached with tanks, He and his men disappeared into the forests as night approached. I was one of a few hundred survivors though half of our men had run off when attacked.

Last of Capitalism

I was posted to Nanjing the next three weeks. Depression set in as I walked the War torn streets of Nanjing. I remember during the 1937 war watching the Japanese Army march into the city. This city has seen wars and wars since ancient times. When the Japanese Army soldiers ran wild killing and raping people in the city I felt weak and helpless. Now the impending invasion of the Left Wing Army is knocking on the wall. There were wild rumors. These wild rumors created havoc on the KMT supporters in this ancient city of Nanjing. They rob Landlords take our land and hand them to their soldiers. Trained by foreign devils from Russia the Gods from Hell are their brothers. Villagers look at each other in suspicion and fear reigns the city.

In the early fighting the KMT Army numbered 3 million and the Communists a tenth of that. But they had controlled the territory outside the city in fact most cities in China. One of the recruiting themes of the Communist Army rang a cold sword into the spines of the wealthy industrialists and massive landowners of the Land.

'All the land and industry of the rich capitalists shall be confiscated when we win victory. Poor people will be given land. Those who join our Armies will receive a minimum allocation of land. This will be the end of capitalism in China all Capitalists shall be put in prison. Support the People's Army, down with Capitalists who profit from corruption.'

Hopelessness and Defeatism kept being repeated in my mind. Our gathering of Sun Tzu's War Strategy club felt despondent, all the signs of victory are with the enemy.

We discussed the results of Battles which had been lost.

In the Campaign at Ankang area which was fought near the, Shanxi Hubei border. Nine divisions of Liu Bocheng's Central Plains Army mounted attacks at General Li Zhengxian's positions. By 17th April Communist troops sacked Zhushan, Zhuxi, Baihe, Xunyang & Pingli.

On July 21st, 27th, 69th & 98th Corps crossed the Han-shui River to the south for a counter-attack.

On Aug 5th, Xunyang-Baihe-Zhushan-Zhuxi-Pingi counties were recovered. But the Huai Hai and Song Sun battles saw a final loss.

A list of Battles we lost was read out.

Battle of Lanzhou

Battle Of Ningxia

Battle of Wuhan

Chiang Kai-shek Frustrating the Army commanders as he countermands decisions in the rapid changing war news. Guangdong-Guangxi Defense was aborted when he Withdrew several armies to Hainan Island. A list of Battles is listed below where the outcomes were bad news.

Battle of Chongqing

Battle of Chengdu

Battle of Quemoy

Defection of Lu Han In Yunnan Province linked with his uncle Long Yun.

On Christmas 1948 we gathered at the Cathedral in Nanjing. It was situated on a hill and we can see the Yangzi River flowing slowly not caring what Armies seek to cross it. We said our prayer to the accompaniment of Christmas carols knowing that evacuation is about to commence. Colonel Chung was there with us.

He said, 'men a big bomber plane is coming to land at the Army Base. We will carry ten truckloads of Chinese treasure to the Base and when it lands in 48 hours we shall load it. '

I protested, 'they rob the National Treasure. Where is it going to land?'

'It is a secret destination a new National Museum probably. Our job is simply load the plane. Understand?'

We worked really hard and everything is ready. But the wait is long.

There is a small middle school next to the base with a lot of music and noise. We drove up the road and joined a school concert in progress.

The lady teacher in pig tails welcomed us after we had donated some money to her students who pestered us for a donation.

'We have a concert about the Great Taiping Rebellion which conquered Nanjing in 1860 to 1864. Come to see our concert you are welcome.'

The Drama teacher a man steeped in history went on stage.

'Ladies and gentlemen and pupils of the school, by coincidence we are staging a play about the fall of Nanjing city in 1864 when the Manchu General Zeng Guo Fan fought against the Emperor of the Taiping Emperor Hung Hsiu Chuan. This ancient city, has witnessed wars for a thousand years. The Taiping rebellion showed the Mad Emperor Hung Hsiu Chuen killing his own deputy then killing himself.'

Madness when he saw starvation in his besieged palace. Madness made him suspect and kill his Deputy Yang Qiuqing. Slowly his kingdom declined in 1862 to 1864.

I am not aware that Hung the mad Emperor was driven mad as he sat in his Palace whilst the Manchu Army besieged it starving the Taiping subjects confined to their fort city. It was the American mercenary F Ward and British soldier Charles Gordon who helped laid charges which blasted a large hole in the Nanjing Eastern Gate Towers.

It started in 1853 when in Kwangsi (Jiangsi) Central China suffered a long drought when millions died of starvation, no food. A Christian teacher and his friend Feng Yun Sang started a small commune which offered starving peasants an orderly commune life. The founders Hong and Feng were Christian converts and organized their commune under 4 Kingdoms of Gods. Farms work hard food plenty..

As the semi Christian semi Chinese commune grew in a China where land was owned by absentee landlords, the Qing or Manchu Emperors sent soldiers to capture the leaders.

They defeated the Manchu General Xiang Rong at Nanjing in 1853 and he killed himself for the defeat.

On May 24, 1852 a Qing gunner fatally wounded Feng as he sat in his sedan chair. This started a revolt and Quanzhou was taken and slaughtered. The Manchu Army numbered 80,000 and the Taiping Rebellion militia force had 460,000, militia. But numbers gave the victory to the Taiping rebel army.

Xiang Rong the Manchu commander committed suicide by hanging himself, or had a fatal overdose of Opium due to wounds. Feng died from a rifle shot of a soldier but Hong's Empire grew with the aid of two able Generals named Yang Qiuqing and Wei Changhui. Constant threats broke them. The Manchu appointed the Marquis Zeng Guo Fan to attack the Taipings which had spread from Kwangsi to Nanjing. Hong became highly suspicious of Yang.

In 1853 Hong Xiuquan disagreed with Yang Xiuqing and became suspicious of Yang's ambitions. Wei Changhui as the Eastern King killed Yang. Their Army is weakened.

Wei in 1856 organized the killing of the East King Yang and 20000 followers.

Zeng Guo Fan appointed an aide a rising General Li Hong Chang who attacked Nanjing. He slowly starved the city. Hong's son, Tiangui Foreign for six weeks. On July 19, 1864, a huge mine blew a long breach in the wall. near the East Gate. The Taiping imperial palace was burned to the ground. About 100,000 soldiers were slaughtered but later estimates of 20 million dead. The teacher well versed in history is probably a socialist for he added the words, 'This rebellion started as a simple food growing commune for starving peasants who had no land. If Feng Yun Shan who never had ambitions to expand had managed to keep the God's little pastures as a starvation heaven for people with no lands it would have been a truly Christian convert haven. But the greed of the Landowners and officials in a corrupt land system, would not tolerate that. Under pressure the Taiping Emperor went mad, Yang the key General went ambitious, and Wei the ambitious plotter staged a coup. This Commander acts with no War strategy. His mind went berserk against the Manchu Army's cruel relentless onslaught. It was fitting that when Manchu Marquis Zeng Guo Fan retired. Whist living in the very same palace that Hong Hsiu Chuan had resided, he was found dead in suspicious circumstances.'

We enjoyed the concert and found it moving. The boredom of waiting for the Super Bomber plane was bad. At last in the night the Plane came. We were surprised to see the Commander in charge. His name was General Chu our old regimental commander during our Battle for Shanghai.

Chung saluted him, 'General is our National Museum going to be closed. These treasures will be lost to China.'

'No silly. We are simply giving it a new home. Mark my words the National Museum in Taiwan is going to be a graceful Palace fit for kings.'

I interrupted him, 'But they belong to China not to Taiwan.'

General Chu chided me, 'Free China is the symbol of the ancient traditions, I shall make sure our new National Museum will be a proud thing a National Treasure.'

As the last of the crates are loaded he saluted us. "You have done a good job. Goodbye may we meet again.'

'Yes sir,' we saluted.

We loaded the National Treasure and saw it flying away in the sky. I realized that China would be ruled by the new government so I wrote a long letter to Grace Lu in Hong Kong releasing her from her promise to be my fiancée. It was not fair for her. The farm that I promised her would probably be seized by the State.

Crossing the Yangzi River

From Nanjing we watched the last Battles of the Civil War fought out. Our Army's front line crumbled before our eyes. After following the news about the three decisive war campaigns the Liaoshen, the Huaihai and the Pingjin campaigns, Colonel Chung lamented, 'all is over, Chiang has lost our war.'

In these last Battles, where the CPC wiped out 144 regular and 29 non-regular KMT divisions, including 1.54 million experienced KMT troops the chance of victory is gone but defeat is probable. This smashed the backbone of the KMT army.

On 21 April, Communist forces crossed the Yangzi. On 23 April, they captured Nanjing, capital of the KMT's Government. Chiang and approximately 2 million Nationalist Chinese retreated from mainland to the island of Taiwan Despite the end of the fighting the two sides have never signed any agreement or treaty to officially end the war. It could be good the hope of a peaceful negotiation, it could be bad a stubborn suicidal heroic fight to the last man.

Slowly the idea of reconciliation was formed that there were 2 China's. By 1954 the famous words by the British Prime Minister

Churchill was coined, 'An iron curtain had been drawn against the face of Eastern Europe and the cold War had begun.'

This surprised many of us as we remembered the four world leaders Churchill, Roosevelt, Stalin and Chiang Kai Shek being photographed laughing together at the Yalta Conference. They were Allies but now are foes.

Colonel Chung and I were lucky for we were sent to a camp but after 6 months we were released into a new world where corruption and land grabs was almost unknown. I hope it can last long.

The next year I retired and lived quietly in Shanghai. Grace Lu wrote to me, 'Gary I may visit you in Shanghai.'

Her letter was timely as I felt very lonely in the cold new world. She came and took me to visit her parents in the Fukien coasts opposite Taiwan. Yes I lived with my old girl friend Grace Lu whom I met in Chungking. We met in Hong Kong and this time in the city of Amoy I went down on my knees and proposed to her. She held me in her arms and said, 'I am your fiancée re-member. Don't worry about the land for I have been gambling in Hong Kong and lost it all. It is when we miss it that it hurts.'

We had a quiet wedding and went on a honey moon to Chungking. Life was good though simple. It was hard living in a new society where everyone was equal.

Future

Such are the epic events and changes which occurred in-side China in the first fifty years of our Twentieth century. Those were our times, these were our leaders. We lived through them, in good times and bad times in peace and in wars. What hap-pens in the second half of the twentieth century? Many Chinese prayed that the glorification of War and the corruption of the Landed Gentry will not be seen ever again.

A seed of greed is forever
Can Power be free of Greed?
Only a rare breed of man
For all times can go uncorrupt.

Sun Tzu's book on the Art of War in Chinese battles retained a special appeal to many who likes the idea of becoming Warlords with supreme powers or just reading about the infamous Warlord era in China when personal survival is a prime factor in the Sino Japanese War. The Sino Japanese Wars seem so far away yet I know it was an interesting part of Chinese history.

The Tea shop which I go regularly is filled with diners as we walked upstairs to a dingy room. There the Sun Tzu study group is filled with the last few members maybe twelve of us. Most of our members fled to Taiwan.

I stood up.

'Members nothing to report the fighting with Taiwan has quieted down. As you know I have resigned from our study group I welcome our new Chairman Colonel Chung and new Sun Tzu adviser Mr. Zhou Hong.'

Young Zhou Hong brought in five new members. He looked confident and bright. With young enthusiasm he grabs Colonel Chung (retired) by the hands and tells us the members, 'Comrades I have to tell you, the Korean War has started. Sun Tzu's predictions are coming true. The North Koreans who invaded South Korea were outflanked by the Americans who landed behind their lines. The encirclement of the North Koreans is too dangerous for the PLA to entertain. As the Americans appeared to advance beyond the Yalu river they will threaten Shenyang the old Manchurian town of Mukden. Sacred unwritten law never attack China's Manchuria. Our troops encircled them and fought them back to the edge of the sea. Then something strange happened. Our Troops voluntarily withdrew back to the old border lines dividing North Korea and South Korea. Some message is inside this withdrawal at the point of victory. What is your view Colonel Gary Tang?'

I said in a tired voice, 'I have no comment I am truly retired as adviser, Zhou. You are our new adviser.'

Colonel Chung murmured, 'The cold war has set in after the second world war. The Russians may intervene on China's side and North Korea had been fighting alongside the Chinese since 1920's against the Japanese occupation of their country. I am afraid Taiwan is hanging in the air waiting for something. It is best to draw a line for peace and negotiate for a stalemate.'

Zhou brightened and said, 'Well we must know that Colonel Gary Tang and Colonel Chung may be retired but in their young days they were veterans of the Nanjing Japanese wars where a great massacre took place. We salute you two old veterans who fought bravely in the Sino Japanese Wars.'

He paused while the small group clapped. There was a long pause. He sipped his tea and then said, 'old wars may go, and new wars may come, but the writings of Sun Tzu on the art of war shall likely go on forever.'

Colonel Chung said, 'I was there in 1937 when the Nanjing Massacre broke out in December January.. Today I have pictures of the slaughter of helpless women, here's the proof.'

I could not believe my eyes. Colonel Chung had taken years to collect these pictures from many sources. It is indelible in our minds the fighting of an ancient war with its savage blind killing occurring in a time warp into the future. This is the future when wars are recorded in pictures taken by cameras by many of the witnesses to a crime. These people lived in those crazy three Months, of war, when 3 million Chinese soldiers fought back inflicting heavy casualties. The Wrath of the Japanese War Demons was awakened. A recall of the Invasion expedition back to Japan is wavering in the minds of the Bureaucrats. It is unthinkable. Somehow somewhere in those hectic chaotic days of October to December 1937 when 300000 lives were slaughtered in an ancient style war there were many camera picture takers including Japanese soldiers, western journalists, pastors and other civilians who snapped the pictures. Now slowly these pictures were collected and shown to the public. Before my eyes were those slaughtered soldiers and civilians who symbolized defiance. Even after the Japanese command had issued orders prohibiting unlawful killings when Nanjing was conquered the soldiers crept through the walls of the Women's refuge to commit rape as if knowing the days of ancient tolerance of killings will soon be prohibited. It was a great horror for me to relive those old days when survival was of prime concern. What horrors the memory of Nanjing Massacre truly haunted me for years. These old wounds were reopened by Chung as he showed us the pictures of horror of the Nanjing Massacres.

Internet Links with sad victim pictures on the Nanjing Massacres are available. See the list below.
1.   http://www.cnd.org/njmassacre/index.html
2.   .http://www.travelchinaguide.com/picture/jiangsu/nanjing/nanjing-massacre/
3.   http://en.wikipedia.org/wiki/Nanking_Massacrehttp://www.cnd.org/njmassacre/
4.   http://www.nanking.com/Photo_pictures_Gallery_exhibition.html
5.   http://thenepalesedebate.forumotion.com/t299-photos-from-the-nanking-massacre
6.   Katsuichi Honda The Nanjing Massacre, Studies of the Pacific Basin Institute,1999
7.   Iris Chang The Rape of Nanking: The Forgotten Holocaust of World War II Penguin 1998